AUTHOR

BAMFORD, S.

TITLE

Walks in South
Lancashire.

SOCIETY AND THE VICTORIANS

WALKS IN SOUTH LANCASHIRE
AND ON ITS BORDERS

SOCIETY & THE VICTORIANS
General Editors: John Spiers
and Cecil Ballantine

The Harvester Press series 'Society & the
Victorians' makes available again important
works by and about the Victorians. Each of the
titles chosen has been either out of print and
difficult to find, or exceedingly rare for many
years. A few titles, although available in the
secondhand market, are needed in modern
critical editions and the series attempts to meet
this demand.

Scholars of established reputation provide
substantial introductions, and the majority of
titles have textual notes and a full bibliography.
Texts are reprinted from the best editions.

Walks in
South Lancashire
and on its borders

with letters, descriptions, narratives,
and observations,
current and incidental

Samuel Bamford

With an introduction by
J. D. MARSHALL
Reader in Regional History, University of Lancaster

THE HARVESTER PRESS 1972

THE HARVESTER PRESS LIMITED
Publishers

50 Grand Parade
Brighton Sussex
BN2 2QA England

'Walks in South Lancashire'
First published in 1844 by the Author

This edition first published in 1972
by the Harvester Press Limited Brighton

Introduction © J. D. Marshall 1972

'Society & The Victorians' No. 5
LC Card No. 77–182735
ISBN 0 901759 23 6

Printed in England by Redwood Press Limited
Trowbridge, Wiltshire
Bound by Cedric Chivers Limited Portway Bath

Contents

CONTENTS

CONTENTS

Introduction

This collection of articles, open letters and fictional studies, written by the famous Lancastrian whose *Passages in the Life of a Radical* (1839–41) has been seen as 'essential reading for any Englishman',[1] is chiefly remarkable for its vivid picture of south-east Lancashire in the age of the Chartists. It was compiled at a time of intense literary activity on Bamford's part, and was preceded by the *Passages*, published in parts, and *Poems* (1843).

It is, indeed, valuable for several reasons. It provides frequent useful reminders that south Lancashire was by no means destroyed by industrialism, even in the vicinity of the great towns. Much of the countryside remained unspoiled until the suburban growth of the present century engulfed it, and its appearance, as Bamford remarked, was that of a 'vast city scattered amongst meads and pastures', even though, as the author admitted, the brooks were often 'discoloured with the refuse of manufactures'. Within the present collection, that

---

[1] E. P. Thompson. *The Making of the English Working Class* (London, 1963), p.836.

series of acutely observed articles entitled 'Walks Amongst the Workers' is a striking, sometimes biased but always independent-minded commentary on the living conditions of industrial families in the area—one which is sometimes at variance with formerly long established notions and abstractions. Bamford's observations serve to remind us that the human scene, even in the 'Bleak Age', was a rich and varied one. Even where he is temperamentally unwilling to look into some social evils which do not serve his case, his articles are valuable for their illustrations of the author's attitude.

His *Walks* commence, physically and in other senses also, at Thornham Fold above Royton (national Grid Reference 896091). For, even before the compilation of these articles was undertaken he lived in the immediate vicinity at Stake Hill, Middleton, between the middle twenties and about 1840; moreover, this was the country of his forbears, and as he tells us in his *Early Days*,[1] his father's grandfather had lived at Hools Wood in Thornham, 'keeping there a small farm, and making cane reeds for weavers of flannel'. In Bamford's time this patch of country-side was one of small hedged enclosures, muddy lanes and low redbrick cottages, scattered about an undulating landscape which hid many a score of weavers or other textile outworkers. Even

---

[1]W. H. Chaloner (ed.) *The Autobiography of Samuel Bamford:Volume One, Early Days* (London, second edition, 1967). p.11.

today, notwithstanding the nearness of the town
of Middleton and the industrial and speculative
building which is transforming the locality, one
can see sections of lane or hamlet (or in
Lancashire parlance, 'fold') which have remained
virtually unchanged since Bamford's time. By
walking on the higher ground near his home, he
could see much of the country which he traverses
in this book, and his *Walks* are largely confined
to an area within a few miles of Thornham
Fold—to Oldham in the south, and to Heywood,
Heap, Rochdale, Crompton, Shaw, Tonge and
Chadderton, a semi-circle of towns and settle-
ments to the north of Oldham itself.

His specialised knowledge of weaving emerges
in his account of Blackley (*Walks,* VIII,
especially p.252 in this book), and he had
apparently worked as a silk weaver during his
residence in the Stake Hill locality. About 1840
he left that district, and settled in a cottage near
Charlestown, Blackley,[1] from which point a
good deal of the material for these articles was
assembled, firmly based on the experiences of
half a lifetime. His visit to Crompton, as a
reference on p.33 shows, seems to have taken
place at some time in 1841, his excursion to
Heywood immediately followed March 1842
(*vide* p.81), while his account of a demonstration
of millworkers (p. 191 and ff.) may well have

---

[1] Ibid, p.24; Dr. Chaloner's biographical and
bibliographical introduction to *The Autobiography*
assembles most of the relevant or known material on
Bamford's life.

been derived from experience of the Plug Riots of 10–11 August 1842, at Royton, Crompton, Lees, Mossley, Hollinwood, Failsworth and Middleton.[1] The last item in the book is dated 24 July 1844, and the author published this collection at Blackley in the same year.

What manner of witness was Samuel Bamford? As Dr Chaloner has pointed out, Bamford's finest years belong to the time of Peterloo, and the rest of his long life was an anti-climax and a period of relative political reaction. At the time of the *Walks* he was vigorously grinding an anti-Chartist axe. Yet this bias does not undermine the integrity of much of his writing, for his fundamental attitudes, which give the latter so much authenticity, are those of a Lancashire rural artisan, proud of the skill, humour and devotion of men like himself, and proud too of his deep local roots and of his distant family connection with a gentry family, the Bamfords of Bamford Hall. His yearning for the supposed rural paternalism of the eighteenth century, typical of so many radicals of his age, led him to idealise the enlightened mill-owner, represented fictionally as Mr Staidley, with his house of 'good English taste' and his reputation as a sort of Sir Roger de Coverley of the manufacturing scene. This attitude may be more significant than may at first appear, because at this very period sections of the industrialist class were (for the

---

[1] A. G. Rose, 'The Plug Riots of 1842', *Trans. Lancs. and Ches. Antiq. Soc.*, 1957, LXVII, pp.99–100.

first time) being appointed in fair numbers to the county magistracy and were establishing themselves as gentle landowners, a new and, to Bamford, meritorious squirearchy.

Although Mr. Staidley may in fact be an amalgam of a number of mill-owners known to the author, his creation could well have been inspired by members of the Fenton family, also of Bamford Hall near Bury. The Fentons, who were bankers as well as industrialists, were associated with Sir James Kay-Shuttleworth through the Congregational Church at Bamford[1] and were, through the firm of Fenton and Schofield, the paternal overlords of the neat industrial colony at Hooley Bridge near Heywood. This last is sympathetically described by the author on p.131, and his description is worth comparing with a similar one on the theme of Hooley Bridge from the pen of a contributor to *The Co-operator* in 1869[2]:

> To the honour of Fenton's family no beerhouse or spirit sellers were allowed at Hooley Bridge. A day school was carried on by order of the worthy firm. There was abundance of spare land about the mill and houses, so that the cottager had his garden to grow vegetables for the family table ... The workpeople of this once happy village were noted as the best housed, best fed, clothed

---

[1] *Victoria County History for Lancashire*, V, p.141, n.80.
[2] *The Co-operator*, No.200, Vol.9, 29 May 1869, p.361.

and educated of any villagers in Lancashire. When the mill ceased to work about seven years ago, the workers in the mill were composed of three generations of the same families.

This model village was evidently a victim of the Cotton Famine, although its physical form remains and can be examined. We must conclude, from this example at least, that Bamford is conceivably a faithful as well as a vivid reporter. But he is not the conveyor of the whole truth. Not all Liberal mill-owners were like his heroes, and a good many artisan Lancastrians were later to vote Tory, some of them apparently in revulsion against the middle-class Liberals who fought factory legislation. The figure of Mr Staidley may indeed be an inspiring one, but the Factory Acts had to be enforced nevertheless.

Bamford, like all reporters and all propagandists, was obliged to select, and inevitably he appears to take a partisan view. His main omissions are not difficult to discern. We are not clearly told, for example, that there is anything very much amiss (apart from some hastily erected housing) with the physical environment of his working family in Heywood (p.85), whose 'floors were clean, the walls white', and whose 'housewife had gotten her week's clothes well washed and hung to dry on lines across the house'. Bamford, after all, has sufficient reason for concentrating on the cleanliness, for his aim throughout is to show the self-reliance, fortitude and patient dignity of the Lancashire worker. As a countryman, he was probably not very interested in smells and dirt,' and we are left to find out for ourselves that the crude death rate in the Bury registration district averaged twenty-five per thousand persons living in the period 1841—51. This level of mortality, not the worst in Lancashire by any means, was connected by Dr. William Farr with 'crowded lodgings — dirty dwellings — personal uncleanliness — the concentration of unhealthy emanations from narrow streets without fresh air, water or sewers'.[1] Thus wrote a propagandist for a different cause. There is plenty of fresh air in Bamford's pages.

Downright omissions are easy enough to deal with; sometimes a more restrained, even objective-seeming passage can mislead more dangerously. Bamford tells us that in Oldham (p.69) 'some of the young people in the carding rooms seemed to suffer from the close air of the place, as was evinced by their sallow complexion and the hoarseness of their voices'. Evidently he could not have known of card-room fever or byssinosis; so, it would seem, he is not the man to tell us about the health of operatives, even though he is here relating the simple truth about what he has seen and heard. But in many other matters he is a valuable guide.

---

[1] *9th Report of the Registrar-General*, 1846, p.26.

WALKS

IN

SOUTH LANCASHIRE,

AND

ON ITS BORDERS;

WITH

LETTERS, DESCRIPTIONS, NARRATIVES, AND OBSERVATIONS,
CURRENT AND INCIDENTAL.

BY SAMUEL BAMFORD.

BLACKLEY, NEAR MANCHESTER:

PUBLISHED BY THE AUTHOR.

1844.

J. HEYWOOD, PRINTER, HEYWOOD.

HOPE!

—

Ah! fair Hope! what a pleasing, but illusive companion hast thou often been to me! Many a bright morning hast thou called me forth, and hast led me by meadow-paths, and through wild-flowers, and wood-gloomings, all echoing bird-songs, and brilliant with dew-pearls. How often hast thou so guiled me forth with thy sweet wind-whispers, telling me we should have a live-long day, all bright, and melodious as that happy hour? How often hast thou told me so? how often have I believed thee? when, alas! a breath of wind; the moving of a vapour; a flash of lightning, hath engloomed heaven, and earth, and marred all thy happy dreams, and mine.

Still thou sayest, "Be of good cheer! remember thy book! 'tis a long night which has no day, a long journey which has no end. Life is full of vicissitude, and shall thine have no change? shall providence, for thine especial persecution exhibit a miracle? think not so; be thou not vain enough to think it. When thou hast done thy work, thou shalt have rest, and not till then. Lag not, therefore, behind now, when the struggle is almost over, when the race is nearly run, and thou art looked for, victorious, at the goal!" Remember, "there is no hill without its dale; no storm without its calm; no shadow without its sun." Come forth then with thy book; cast it on the waters, it will be to thee and others, a blessing! live, and be thankful.

Ah! fair Hope! I am thankful; thankful for the humblest of God's gifts, and my book is one of them. Thankful am I also, for thy words of advice, but I dare not cast my book upon the waters. No, fair Hope; one sop in the mouth is worth two in the mill-pond.

Encouraged however, by thee, I again venture forth, my little pen-work in hand. The booksellers I cannot deal with largely, the sops being too few for both them and me. I must, therefore, as hath been my wont, do much of my business myself, and sell my pen-work wherever I can find a market.

To my humble brothers of the anvil, the loom, and the jenny, will I offer it; and they will read it, well pleased, when they have sat down from their night-toil, and have wiped the sweat from their brow, and have partaken the homely meal. It will be to them, what thou, Oh Hope, hast been to me; a comforter in adversity; a star in mid-gloom; a well in their desert journey; a soother of life; a putter-away of evil broodings.

I will tender it unto the dealer who sells food from behind his counter; to the dark-vested, hard-handed son of crispin; to the apothecary, who dispenses anodynes for whining children, it will keep even him awake; to the manufacturer, who, "reduces wages," as well as to him who pays them honourably; to the warehouseman, who, enquiring after knowledge, nightly associates with others for instruction, with him it may beguile an hour, stolen from more severe reflections. The man of law shall behold my book. To the door of his closet will I venture, where he sits amidst wills, writs, conveyances, and bankrupt commissions: I will fear not his grave and learned look through his glasses, though his eye do scan me with the plain fore-question,—"who can this be? this is no client of mine, why comes he here?" also that most useful and industrious, dumb-sitting, back-bending, and knee-cramping man, who makes our clothes, shall hear my footstep on his stair, and peruse my little ·inimitable, when, o'nights, he has time to stretch his limbs. The tradesman who buys and sells, to me will be a buyer. If Webster and company offered him their Calicoes yesterday, why may not I offer him my prints to day; my living, moving, soul-vivid prints; my dyes of human life. The merchant too shall have my book laid before him. He may look at it, turn it over, and haggle a little, if he choose, but he also will buy; aye! and read, and buy more for his friends in the south country. " Hast thou anything to do? do it thyself," says Poor Richard; even so will I do my business myself, and sell my book. The clergy, I know, will be readers of mine: they are always glad to see individuals of the humble class rising up to do good. They never forget, that their Lord and Master was one of "our order;" they are friends to instruction; to the enlightenment and enlargement of mind, and most especially will they patronize a book penned by one who learned to make letters at a sunday school. Wesleyans will hail, with joy, the "one sinner that hath repented." Catholics will absolve me, having humbly confessed. Friends will, no doubt, tender me the hand of friendship; whilst nobles, statesmen, judges, and legislators of our land, will read my book with deep thought and reflection, beholding therein, a kind of indicator; a whisper of the rising wind; a ripple of the coming tide; a footstep before the tramping of the multitude which is putting on the shoe, and binding the latchet, before it sets forth, to tread over the whole land.

May God so direct the hearts of our rulers and law-makers, that they may be disposed to meet this universal movement of mind, whilst it is yet of mind only; in a spirit of justice, and of peace, such as shall make the honest labourer contented, and rescue him from the influence of designing and incendiary agitators. May they at last relent, and permit him to have that for which he bowed to the primeval curse— bread, for the sweat of his toil. And may our gold-exalted great ones, whether of the land or of manufacture, also come forward as liberators, ere the pent up souls, and down-bended bodies of their toiling ones, rise up, and rush forth with the mad joy of cage-broken wolves.

May they, whilst it is yet in time, "loose the band of wickedness, and undo the heavy burdens, and let the oppressed go free, and break every yoke."

And "may the Lord then guide them continually, and satisfy their souls in draught, and make fat their bones, and may they be like a watered garden, and like a spring of water whose water fails not."

And "may they that be of them, build the old waste places; may they raise up the foundations of goodness, in the hearts of many generations; may they be called the repairers of the breach, the restorers of paths to dwell in." So be it.

SOUTH LANCASHIRE.

WHAT a naturally fine country is this SOUTH
LANCASHIRE! and what an interesting people inhabit
it! let us approach nearer, as it were; let us cast an
observant eye over the land; let us note the actions,
and listen to the conversation of the people, and endeavour to express in writing, our impressions as to
both the country and its inhabitants.

From Liverpool to Manchester, the land is generally
level, and is almost wholly applied to agriculture; but
in traversing the country from Manchester to Tod-
morden, which is on the extreme northern verge of
the district, probably not one mile of continuously
level ground will be passed over. Betwixt Bury on
the western, and Oldham, on the eastern verge, some
comparatively level tracts are found, as those of
Radcliffe, Whitemoss, and Failsworth; but they are
small as compared with the distance, and all the remaining parts of this northern district, are composed
of ups and downs, hillocks, and dells, bent, twisted,

and turned in every direction. Take a sheet of stiffened paper for instance, crumple it up in your hand,
then just distend it again, and you will have a pretty
fair specimen of the surface of the northern part of
South Lancashire. The hills are chiefly masses of
valuable stone and coal; on the north, some heath-
lands overlap them, but their sides are often brilliant
with a herbage that yields the best of milk and butter,
whilst of all the valleys, you shall traverse none, where
a stream of water does not run at your side, blabbing
all manner of imaginary tidings, and asking unthought
of, and unanswerable questions. To be sure, during
six days out of the seven, the brooks, and lowland waters, are often turgid and discoloured with the refuse of
manufactures; but, steal along one of these quiet dells
on a Sunday morning, go over the shallows, where the
loaches used to lie basking, and look into the deeps,
and quiet pools, and shady spots, where the trout were
wont to be found, creep under the owlers, and through
the hazels, when their golden blossoms are hung in
the sun; go plashing among the willows, and over the
hippin-stones, and along the gravel-beds, where the
pebbles lie as white as hail turned to stone. Go
maundering, solitary and thoughtful, for an hour or
two, amid these lonely haunts, and you shall confess
that our county is not reft of all its poetry, and its
fairy dells, and its witching scenes.

Then, the meadows and fields spread fair and green
betwixt the towns. Clean, sleek milk-kine are there,

licking up the white clover, and tender grass. Small farms are indicated by the many well-built, and close-roofed homesteads, contiguous to which are patches of potatoe, corn, and winter food for cattle. A farmer's man is never met with here, whose cheek does not shew that he lives far above want, and that, if he dines not on delicacies, he feeds on rude plenty.

The smoke of the towns and manufactories is somewhat annoying certainly, and at times it detracts considerably from the ideality of the landscape ; but, bad as it is, it might have been a great deal worse; for we may observe that the smoke only goes one way at one time ; that the winds do not divide and scatter it over all the land : it sails far away in streams, towards the north, east, west, or south, and all the remainder of sky, and hill, and vale, are pure and cloudless.

From the top of one of the moor-edges, Old Birkle, for instance, on a clear day, with the wind from the south west, we may perceive that the spaces betwixt the large towns of Bury, Bolton, Manchester, Stockport, Ashton, Oldham, Rochdale, Middleton, and Heywood, are dotted with villages, and groups of dwellings, and white detached houses, and manufactories, presenting an appearance somewhat like that of a vast city scattered amongst meads and pastures, and belts of woodland; over which, at times, volumes of black furnace clouds go trailing their long wreaths on the wind.

Such is the appearance of the country to the east and south of where we stand, (Old Birkle) whilst the aspect of that to the west and north, is more strongly marked by nature, being ridged with high moor-land hills, dark and bleak; and furrowed by deep vallies and precipitous dells, which are swept by brooks, and mill streams, and enlivened by nooks of evergreen pasture, and groups of cottages, and far detached dwellings. Here also is generally found, the eternal money-making-mill, the heart-work, the life-organ, the bread-finder, and the deformity of the place.

The inhabitants are a mixture of Celts, Saxons, and Norse-men, or Danes; but the Saxon blood is supposed to predominate, and it may be affirmed with certainty, that Saxon is prevalent in the dialect of the rural population. The name of nearly every hill, valley, stream, or homestead, is Celtic or Saxon, and of the old families, perhaps, a still greater proportion are designated in Saxon terms.

The population may be divided into three classes; the monied—the middle—and the labouring classes. The former we will suppose to comprise all persons of independent property, whether they be engaged in trade or otherwise;—the middle, includes tradesmen, manufacturers, shopkeepers, and masters in every branch of industry;—and the working class, will, of course, consist of such as labour daily to supply the necessaries of life. The first class are here more numerous than in any other equal space of ground out of Middlesex, and probably they are more wealthy than any other equal number of persons, residing in any one district of the same extent—the above excepted—on the whole earth. They are therefore vastly powerful, so far as money can make them so. In matters of trade, exports, imports, profit, and loss, their information cannot be exceeded. In the management of banking concerns they are not so acute, as has recently been shewn; they have been too credulous of plausibility; the rise in life, of many of them, seeming almost a miracle, they have been the more disposed to believe in other miracles, and so became deceived. In politics, they, as a body, are but new beginners; and it is but lately that leaders of ability in their own rank, have sprung up amongst them.

Some of them still appear to consider politics as a forbidden theme, and are vastly sensitive if such subjects are introduced, even in connection with matters, the very essentials of which are political, but the number of these fastidious gentlemen is becoming less, as common sense comes more into use. The prejudice has been rather clung to, in consequence of the strong feelings which have too often characterized political advocacy in this neighbourhood; some exhibitions of the sort occupy a place in history, and though scenes and actors pass away, impressions remain which are a long time in wearing out.

• When we find members of this monied class acting in bodies, we see them perform nobly; their time, their labour, and their money are given profusely; and this, the ministers of religion, the promoters of public institutions, and the leaders of any movement where wealth and energy are required, know, and they take their measures accordingly. In their individual characters, members of this class evince less promptitude; not, probably, because they are less inclined to act, but because they wish to know what others are prepared to do; they seem to be shy of leading, save in matters of trade, and hence they act better in public, as a class, than as individuals.

The middle class is still more numerous than is the monied, and the remark with respect to the wealth of the former may be applied here. In politics they are better informed, and more public-spirited; more honest also, and more zealous in the support of their several views of things. As a body, they are perhaps unequalled for general information, as well as for talent in the application of it to public uses. Of all municipal matters, they are the life and soul. In literature, they are far before the monied class; and liberally patronise resident talent; they number among them many who are eminent in science; many who are patrons of, and no mean proficients in the fine arts; whilst music is becoming to them a passion, oratory a relaxation, and poetry a great favourite.

And what shall I say of the working class?

That they are the most intelligent of any in the island—in the world. The Scotch-workers are the only ones who approach them in intelligence; they are the greatest readers; can shew the greatest number of good writers; the greatest number of sensible and considerate public speakers. They can shew a greater number of botanists; a greater number of horticulturists; a greater number who are acquainted with the abstruse sciences; the greatest number of poets, and a greater number of good musicians, whether choral or instrumental. From the loom they will bring out any thing that has ever been worked in Europe; in mechanics they are no-where surpassed, and in mining take rank with the best. They probably turn out a greater amount of work than any other equal number of people under the sun. They are ardent in temperament, which helps them to support their heavy labour, but which also tends to lead them into ill considered schemes and projects, and into the traps and snares of designing political quacks. Being of honest intention themselves, they have seldom paused to examine the pretensions of those who sought to become their leaders; hence they have been miserably duped. The late Henry Hunt was the first who obtained their blind devotion: some of his distinguished followers also shared his popularity, but of those, Hunt, as is well known, was jealous, and if any co-patriot received more attention than the leader liked to spare, he kicked the aspirant, or tried to do so, and there was a feud; his own train, however, at last dwindled into something more like a country stang-riding than a gathering of radicals.

After him followed successive contentions about

wages. Combinations, conspiracies, and turn-outs, came in their turn, and some of them were stained with blood. Each event had its leader, who for the time, occupied a share of the public notice. Then came the three glorious days, and parliamentary reform, and when O'Connell deemed it needful to whisk off a joint or two from his tail, he did so, and Mr. Feargus O'Connor appeared on our stage. He has tried to enact the English Hunt, and the Irish O'Connel over again before us, and he has failed in both characters; not having the nerve of the one, nor a tithe of the talent of either. Latterly, he has been holding forth about the purchase of land, by a class who cannot entirely purchase bread; just at present, I understand, he is experimenting amongst the colliers: and thus the miserable deluder is hastening through life to find himself, at last, deluded.

At present, there is not amongst our workers any political leader, in whom is united any considerable share of their confidence. Joseph Sturge has made one or two efforts that way, but he is not the man to walk at the head of this people. He is, I think, too amiable, and too honest,—although a little, meekly vain perhaps—for the trade of a demagogue. He may be useful in some way however, and I doubt not he will endeavour to be so; but assuredly he is not calculated for a mob-rider.

Meanwhile the seed, which from time to time has been sown, whether of tares or of corn, is germinating amongst a thoughtful people : the advancement is silently at work, down in the coal mines, up in the factories, abroad in the fields, far o'er the moors, and close by in the cottages : the ground is moving with emotion ; the moral atmosphere is thickening with words, and thoughts, and silent expressions, more significant than words. All are moving, in some manner or other, forward ! forward ! There is no turning back. And when this motion becomes united in one stream, to which it is daily tending, what shall resist it ? whither shall it go ? how shall it end ?

And is this tendency to be wondered at ? The people are born in masses, we may almost say ; they live in masses ; they work in masses ; they drink in masses ; they applaud in masses ; they condemn in masses ; they joy in masses ; they sorrow in masses ; and, as surely as that Etna will vomit fire, they will, unless they be wisely and timely dealt with, some day, act in masses.

I do not undertake to say that here is a power capable alone, of disarranging the present order of things ; but I do say that I am of opinion, that here, in time will be found, mind sufficient to conceive, and will—aided by circumstances—to give the first impulse to a movement, the like of which has not been known in England. These explosive elements—ever increasing—cannot be continually tampered with, without producing their result.

If God has bestowed upon me some little ability,

and by his own ways of adversity, led me to dwell amongst this people, one of them, and still apart,—having thoughts, and ways, and views of my own;—loving all that should be loved, and despising only the despicable,—if he has so fortified my heart by severe experience, that I can judge in charity, and disapprove without anger; that I can support the right without wishing to retaliate in wrong; that I would feed the hungry without robbing the plenteous; that I would free the enslaved, without enchaining their task-masters; that I would mitigate asperities, and promote kindly regards amongst all classes: if my Creator has given me a heart to wish these things, and a head to labour for their accomplishment, or any part of it, shall I not evince my gratitude to Him, by exercising the little talent he has bestowed? Assuredly so. And if, as the greatest reformer and patriot that ever lived, once said, " Blessed are the peace-makers," may it be my endeavour to deserve a place,—however humble—amongst those blessed.

B

WHAT SHOULD BE DONE ?

FRIEND ACRELAND,

You ask my opinion as to what should be done in the present state of the country. You seem to have a kind of fore-boding of some great change shortly to take place, and you are pretty much of my way of thinking, as to the part the people, —the working classes—are likely to take during such change, should it occur. How they are likely to conduct themselves during the transaction; and what should be done, to render them instrumental for good, instead of evil, when the time arrives, seem to be the main questions of your letter, and I will, if you please, confine my reply to the second question. "What should be done?" the other depends entirely on it, and may be shortly answered. The people are likely to conduct themselves, during any great change that may occur, exactly as they have been instructed to conduct themselves; or, in other words, as they have cause to conduct themselves; therefore the question is, "What should be done?"

This is a momentous question, friend Acreland; you do me no small honour by asking my opinion upon it; and to yóu, I will frankly give it, because I know you will receive it in the same spirit of candid sincerity in which it is tendered ; that spirit which is always essential to a useful correspondence, will undoubtedly benefit us both in our present enquiry; and with such mutual good-will, we may proceed.

You ask, " What should be done ? " and I reply, the working people—the masses—should be cultivated. That, in my opinion, is what should be done.

Oh ! methinks I hear you say, " we are doing that, you know, we are instructing them. You must have read in the papers how the dissenters are stirring in the cause ; what noble donations they have given ; and you cannot have overlooked the meeting lately held in Manchester, of the members and friends of " The Church Education Society." You must have heard of these proceedings."

I have heard of them, dear Acreland ; I have read the details in the newspapers, and have been greatly interested by the reading. I have been much pleased to see even these movements, greatly short though they fall, of the purposes one might have expected from such high quarters. I could expatiate most disparagingly, but I wont ; my task being to shew what should be done, rather than what is purposed to be done, and the inefficiency of the purpose.

The people then, I say—emphatically—should be

cultivated, and your education schemes, good, and well intended as they are, do not go that length.

"Why, what would you have? again you say. What is cultivation but instruction, education, training up of the mind?"

Oh, cultivation, my friend, is a little more than that. The Irish tell us they are the most learned people in the world; that their bog-cutters speak the dead languages; the Scotch say they are the best educated, but I believe neither the one nor the other; and if both were true, our people here want something more than either; they want cultivation, and that, you know, begins with succour. They must be fed.

"Oh, but your cultivation is likely to lead a great way then."

Still further, good Acreland. They must be fed; they must be clothed; they must be sheltered; and how is all this to be accomplished? they must be employed; aye! and paid for their employment.

After you have thus cultivated their outward life, you will find but little difficulty in winning their inner life to any thing which is reasonable and proper. If you really care for their well-being, they will soon find it out,—you need not make a parade of your sympathy. Was there ever a class of sentient beings in the world which did not, in some way or other, evince a regard for their benefactors? Certainly not. And does any reason exist which might lead us to suppose, that man is less grateful than other animals? Certainly not. Try the experiment then. Feed our people; clothe them; shelter them; or in other words, employ them; pay them; and give them an opportunity for feeding, clothing, and sheltering themselves. Watch over their interests; be regardful of their worldly welfare; help the feeble; vindicate the oppressed; comfort the sorrowful; relieve the destitute. Do these things, and I may defy all the fire-brand demagogues that ever flared away at torch-light meetings, to estrange one heart from its affection towards you and your order.

Above all things, be just towards them in respect of their civil rights, and fear not. You need not hesitate, they will never be like a French mob. There is more of an aristocratic spirit in the commonalty of England, than any other people; there is indeed too much of it. They are as regularly stratified, as are the the rocks of our island, and they wont be disrupted, except by great, and long continued ill usage. Oh ! no, no, they wont be elbowed out of their place by a trifle; they wont stand that, nor do they wish to mount into yours, you may depend upon it. They want none of your fineries, nor your sumptualities, nor your knackeries of big babyism; they rather contemn those things, but they do want what they have a right to have, a good living for their right good labour; aye ! and they will have it too, either with labour or without it. Let them have their cottages then, with their bright warm hearths in winter—let them have their neat gardens, with flowers, and spring herbs and potatoe plats : let those in towns have money where-with to purchase from the baker, and the butcher, and the butter maid, and the herb seller, that they may have broth on sundays, and, good hash 'or hot-pie on week days, with something left for a gown or a shirt, or duds for the little ones, when they are wanted. In short, live, and let live, and stand aside for once, and ever, that God's sun-shine may fall on other hearts than your own. Do these things, friend Acreland ; that is, let your order do them, and Oh! I need not say how very easily all your and our difficulties would be overcome.

Then, my dear friend, you might begin to instruct us at railway speed. We should drink it all in, and never forget the lessons given by those we loved. Our hearts, teeming with grateful emotions, would be like ground prepared for every good seed, and you might sow and cultivate a harvest, at which angels might weep with joy. Oh, what a glorious work is spread before the great ones of our land, if they would but perform it, or would but lend aid that others might do it for them.

Will they do this, friend Acreland ? I believe you would if you could, but will your order take up the good work ? Will they plow down the old sour sods of prejudice, and selfishness, and ignorance, and turn up the new mould, which has long been waiting to give forth—to God's glory and man's benefit,—all the riches, and blessings with which it is endowed.

Still, the subject is not exhausted; we have agreed, I will suppose, that, " the people should be cultivated," in order to which, " they should be employed." Then the question arises, how is employment to be found for them ? and the answer to that will explain my views with respect to their physical cultivation, and the means for that end. We may afterwards discuss the subject of their mental cultivation ; but for the present, perhaps enough has been advanced.

Adieu ! dear Acreland. I shall be happy to hear from you again ; and still more so to learn that you have become a convert to the opinions of,

Yours most truly,

SAMUEL BAMFORD.

To THOMAS ACRELAND, GENT.
Sperrington Grange,
North Lancashire.

WALKS AMONGST THE WORKERS.

THE condition of the working classes, physically, morally, and mentally, having of late begun to attract that degree of attention which it ought long ago to have done, I conceived that, at this particular crisis, some good might be rendered to the country—some advancement made towards the Truth—by an actual survey of the present condition of such labouring persons. I determined therefore, on taking a series of perambulations amongst them, for the purpose of noting down their real state and condition, and of making it known through the public press of the country.

The course which I marked out for myself in the performance of this self-imposed but important task, was to obtain the best information I could from persons supposed capable of giving it; to converse with the employers, wherever I found them accessible, as well as with the employed; to notice the latter at their dwellings and at their places of labour—in their hours of rest as well as at their daily toil—and generally, whilst I sought information from others, from men and women of all classes and conditions, not to omit any opportunity for the exercise of my own observation. With the effect, however feeble, which my notices might have on a great question of the day—with their tendencies for or against the doctrines of contending parties—I conceived that I had nothing to do; the elucidation of the simple truth, for its own sake, and the good which accompanies it, being the only object of my solicitude.

Directing my steps to the northward of my dwelling, I first paused on gaining the summit of the highway across the township of Thornham, near Middleton, and looking around, I felt that a few minutes would not be mis-spent in glancing over the bold and interesting scene which was spread out before me. Going forth to note the brief joys and sorrows of my fellow-man, could I feel less than admiration and thankfulness at the prospect of the goodly land which his beneficent Creator had spread out for his habitations. To the west are the hills and moors of Crompton, the green pastures year by year, cutting further up into the hills; the ridge of Blackstone-edge, with Robin Hood's bed, darkened as usual by shadows; whilst the moors, sweeping round to the left, (the hills of Calder-moor, Whitworth, and Wuerdle) bend somewhat in the form of a shepherd's crook around a fair and sunny vale, through which the Roche flows past cottages, farms, and manufactories. Such is the scene before us, fair and lovely at a distance, mute to the ear and tranquil to the eye—like a cradle below the hills, where the bright day reposes amid sweet airs and cooling streams. So much for the landscape before us; now then, for the closer realities of our task.

The colliery of Messrs. Wilde, Andrew, and Co., at Addershaw, or Hathershaw, or Heathershaw, first claims our inspection. The shaft is about a hundred yards in depth, the coal about forty-two inches in thickness, and some of the coals extend to the distance of eleven hundred yards from the shaft; the coal is wound up by a perpetual chain, which works admirably. The men are paid by "the quarter," which contains fifteen loads, or thirty baskets, or sixty hundred weight of coal; for this they get three shillings and nine-pence, with three-pence added for every hundred yards they have to waggon the coal to the shaft; so that a man working close to the shaft receives three shillings and nine-pence for his quarter, he who works one hundred yards off, gets four shillings, one working at two hundred yards, four shillings and three-pence, and so in proportion. The price of coal at the pit is seven-pence halfpenny per basket, a very reasonable price in comparison with some necessaries. A man at full work would get eight quarters of coal in six days, and his wages for them would be one pound ten shillings, besides the allowance of three-pence per hundred yards for waggoning.

The man workiug at a distance from the shaft has generally a stout lad to waggon for him, and the lad's wages are one-third of whatever the collier gets. A man, therefore, who gets his eight quarters, and pays a waggoner, will have twenty shillings for himself, and he who does without a waggoner, will have his thirty shillings. These earnings would, one is apt to suppose, be a pretty comfortable thing for the cottage of a working man. Colliers, however, such is the nature of their employment, can hardly be too well paid, and, unfortunately, we have something else to take into consideration. The men are now, both at this and the adjoining colliery, compelled to work "short time," a short but expressive phrase which we meet with at nearly every step. They are paid fortnightly, and sometimes, of late, they have only been allowed to get six quarters in the fortnight. The cause is want of sale, in consequence of the neighbouring factories working short time also: the good brisk sale which they formerly had, "is gone out of this side of the country;" it is only about two-thirds of what it used to be, and the falling off in employment is proportionate.

Several wives and children came to the pits with the men's dinners; they mostly carried a small tin can with a lid on, and a ring to hold it by. Some would bring the victuals in a pot basin, tied in a napkin, or pinned in a bit of clean rag. I felt a curiosity to know what the poor, panting, toiling fellows in the dark mine had to sustain them, but I could not make up my mind to ask the women to let me see of what their humble supply consisted; a banksman at Hanging Chadder (the next colliery) informed me that the men generally got boiled milk and loaf for their dinner, at their work; sometimes they might have potatoes and a little flesh-meat, and sometimes they would get potatoes and salt only, and very seldom was it, he said, that they had any ale at meals. I must own I was disappointed in this bill of fare; I had expected that these men would be living on good substantial food, as they ought to do; I had not supposed that a collier could sustain his most laborious and horrid toil without plenty of highly nourishing food, but I thus found it otherwise. Well might the poor women look half sorrowful, half ashamed, as I thought some of them did, when they handed the uncheering meal to the banksman; they cast an averted glance as it descended, and then hurried away. I did not hear of any dissatisfaction against the coal-masters—their rate of wages is probably as good as any in the district; the complaints were against the shortness of work, occasioned by the low demand for coal.

We are now at a place called Gravel Hole, a fold or hamlet of some fifty brick houses, situated on an elevated site in the township of Thornham. About twelve or fourteen years since, these houses were all inhabited by fustian hand-loom weavers; they are now occupied, one or two excepted, by fustian cutters.

The old inhabitants have gone down into the vallies to work at the factories, and the present residents are new-comers from many parts of the country—from Manchester, from Lymm in Cheshire, and from Yorkshire. The master cutters, I am informed, make a good living here; they are supposed to earn from thirty to thirty-four shillings per week. A young boy or girl, working journey-work, will get from seven to nine shillings, by five days' labour. They work, four or five together, in the old loom-shops and the chambers, and form very agreeable company, wiling away their monotonous employment by singing in a very pleasing manner, in concert, snatches of popular songs, or religious pieces. The rent of a house with a shop which formerly held four looms, and with present convenience for about twelve cutting-frames, is six pounds; and eight shillings for poor rates, and one shilling for highway rate; the firing of course is very cheap, not in any case probably exceeding one shilling a week. Every house is now occupied, and the fustian cutters are, as we have seen, not in a condition to make complaint.

At Narrow-head-Brow, whither I turned instead of going into the valley of the Roche, I found some hand-loom weavers employed on toilonett, a neat light cloth, made of black cotton warp, and shot with white woollen yarn in hank. It is about an eighteen hundred reed, thirty-two inches in width, and the pieces or cuts are thirty yards in length; the shoots from one hundred and eighty, to two hundred in the inch. A weaver will be four days in dressing his warp, and about eight in weaving a cut, and his wages will be seventeen shillings, including the charge for winding, and sow, or paste for dressing, which if we reckon at two shillings and sixpence, will leave his actual gain about seven shillings and three-pence per week. The cloth is made for the Yorkshire market; it is dyed and finished for cloaks, and some of it is probably used for Macintosh cloth. The rents here are about four pound ten shillings to five pounds, for a four-loomed house, with all rates, probably making ten shillings more. The condition of these hand-loom weavers—the remnant of the old fustian weavers—is not so comfortable as that of the fustian cutters last described. Several houses were unoccupied; others in a state of partial dilapidation; garden fences were broken down, and the gardens had become grass plats. The interior of the dwellings were not so comfortable nor well ordered as the last I had seen; the poor occupants were not by any means uncleanly or slovenly, but they seemed to be contending against necessities, which left them small leisure for thinking of niceties in dress or furniture.

At High Crompton, the factory hands were all returning from dinner to their work. I noticed them particularly, and did not observe one, of either sex, who was not decently and cleanly attired. Some of the young men and women were very respectably dressed, for their station; and, with but few exceptions, all the hands appeared to be healthy. One of the principal manufacturers at Shaw coming up the street, I stated to him, candidly, the motive for my visit to this part, and expressed a hope, that when I called at his mill, as I probably should, no difficulty would be experienced by me in endeavouring to ascertain the actual condition of his workpeople. He said there would be no difficulty, but seemed to think that the best information might be obtained from the overseer of the poor, and the collector of rates, the latter of whose address he gave. I said I should be glad to avail myself of whatever information they could afford, but must at the same time make use of my own observation as much as possible. After parting from this gentleman, I called on Mr. J, C., a manufacturer at this place, to whom I explained the nature of my visit, as before. He readily entered into my views, and without the least hesitation took me into his counting house, and shewed me his book of the wages he paid to his spinners and weavers. He employed about one hundred and sixty hands, spun thirties counts, and paid from two shillings and sixpence to two shillings and eightpence per thousand hanks. His mules were of the largest size and newest construction, running four hundred and eighty spindles each, and one spinner, with two piecers, would superintend two mules, or nine hundred and sixty spindles. The spinner would get from three pound ten shillings, to four pound seven shillings in fifteen days, and the average of his earnings would be three pound eighteen shillings and six-pence in the same time, and of this he would have to pay his piecers seven shillings a week each, that would be one pound eight shillings in the fortnight, and it would leave him one pound ten shillings, of clear gain, or fifteen shillings a week. Mr. C. employed sixty-seven power-loom weavers of cords and velveteens. The weavers generally superintended two looms each, several had three looms, and one or two had four looms, the latter being assisted tenters, whom they had to pay. A weaver of average ability, would earn, on two looms, from ten to twelve shillings per week; one with three looms, would get from thirteen to fourteen shillings; and one with four looms, would earn as much as fifteen shillings a week clear. A number of the hands lived in houses belonging to Mr. C., for which they paid from one shilling and sixpence, to two shillings and nine-pence per week, and their rent was settled every pay day. I made excuses to enter some of the houses, and found them uniformly neat and clean, one tenement was beautifully clean; the walls were as white as lime could make them; the good housewife, who was up to the elbows in suds, gave me liberty to see her chambers, and I found the walls and the beds on a par with the house below; they were almost spotless, and the air was as untainted as the wind. This was one of a row of houses; several others which I entered were almost in as good condition; they had generally flowers and green shrubs in the windows, and before the doors were small gardens with flowers and a few pot herbs. The tenements consisted of a front room, a kitchen, and two chambers, and the front rooms were furnished with handsome fire-grates, ovens, and boilers, all as well burnished as black lead, a good brush, and a willing hand could make them. The rent of these dwellings was two shillings and nine-pence per week, clear of all rates. At another house which I visited I found a dame-school. A young married woman sat with about a dozen fine, cleanly, and healthy looking children around her. She learned them reading, knitting, and sewing, and charged from three-pence to four-pence a week; but complained that the factories working short time had deprived her of many scholars. *

At the village of Shaw I readily found the overseer, the collector of rates, and the registrar of births and deaths, each of whom, with the greatest frankness, communicated to me such facts as lay within his respective province. I am sorry to say that the gentleman, the manufacturer whom I have mentioned as having met at High Crompton, did not, any more than his partners, evince an equal willingness to oblige me. One of these persons, as a preliminary question, asked who paid me, and expressed his belief that I must be employed by " some government spy !" The gentleman first alluded to, when asked to inform me what wages he gave his workmen? said he thought he

c

* This was in the year 1841.

had given me ample reference for my purpose, in directing me to the overseer and the collector of rates. Had I not seen the collector ? I said I had, and he had given me all the information he could. Well, and was not that sufficient ? did it not show the distress of the township ? I said it did, but that was not what I was looking after; I wished to ascertain the actual condition of the labouring population, in order to which I must have a knowledge of their earnings. Perhaps, he said, I wished to ascertain their prosperity ? No, I said, I wished not to ascertain either their prosperity or their distress; I wished to know their actual condition only; I had nothing to do with party questions. Well, he could not see what good could arise from an enquiry so directed. I said he must allow me to judge on that point myself, but as there seemed to be some reluctance to afford the information, I should not press for it, and so I left him.

From the three public officers before-mentioned, I learned that the township of Crompton, of which Shaw is the principal village, was two and a half miles in length, and two in breadth, comprising about two thousand one hundred and forty-four statute acres; that its population, in one thousand eight hundred and thirty-one, was—six thousand nine hundred and ninety-three; and in one thousand eight hundred and forty-one—six thousand seven hundred and twenty-four; that the number of inhabited houses, was one thousand two hundred and twenty-six, uninhabited, two hundred and twelve; that there were twenty-one public-houses in the township, and twenty-three cotton manufactories six of which were stopped; that there were two schools at which reading, writing, and arithmetic were taught; several day schools at which factory children were instructed, and eight sunday schools, at four of which writing was taught; that the number of families relieved from the poors' rate was seventy-five, and the number of persons relieved on an average, four hundred and ninety-two. The amount paid to the poor fortnightly, was about twenty-five pounds. The amount of poors' rate in one thousand eight hundred and forty, was—one thousand nine hundred and fifteen pound, seven shillings and fourpence halfpenny, and it would be as heavy this year; the amount of uncollected rates at present, was sixty-eight pounds fourteen shillings and eleven-pence, exclusive of rates which had been remitted to some of the poorest inhabitants. The collector said he had been in office six years, and he never knew the rates so difficult to collect as at present; it arose from the factories working short time. They had been continually working short time during the last six months, until a week or two of late, when they again commenced working full time. The mill-workers in general were not so very badly off, but many who appeared in comfortable circumstances as working people, were actually distressed. There was not a pawn-shop in the township, but many of the necessitous people went to Oldham and Royton to pledge articles. Many ratepayers, who, five years since, always paid their rates on the first application, now could not pay, and he had to call upon them many times. The licensed victuallers were frequently transferring their houses; the business was not a steady or a profitable one. There was no mechanics' institute—no public library —no reading room, except one supported by chartists —nor any bookseller's or stationer's shop in the place. I also ascertained, from various sources, that it is customary to have provision shops connected with the mills. These shops were not conducted in the master's name, but were superintended by the family of an overlooker, or a relative of the master manufacturer (as in one instance, where the master's brother kept the shop) Those workmen who bought their necessaries at these shops were generally in steady employment, whilst those who, through previous engagement, or a wish to better themselves, went elsewhere, were not so sure of employment. The prices of articles at a shop not connected with a mill were as follow:—Flour, two shillings and sixpence per dozen; meal, one shilling and seven-pence per dozen; malt, two shillings per peck; hops, one shilling and fourpence per ℔.; butter, (Irish,) eleven-pence per ℔.; cheese, seven-pence halfpenny per ℔.; bacon, seven-pence to eight-pence per ℔.; and potatoes, one halfpenny per ℔, I had not an opportunity of ascertaining what the prices were at the mill shops, but was informed that it is well understood, that articles may be purchased for less money at the shops not belonging to the mills, and very often of better quality.

THE TRAVELLER.

———

IT was on the afternoon of a day in the month of November, that a stranger, travelling on foot, entered the little inn at the village of Webster-dyke, in the well known district of South Lancashire. He was, apparently, about the age of thirty years, of a tall and sinewy form. He wore a drab coat, buttoned tight at the waist, cord breeches, kersey gaiters, and stout, well thonged shoes; a brown spotted silk neck-kerchief was neatly tied below his white shirt collar, a black beaver hat, seemingly new, was on his head, and he carried a knotted crab-stick in his hand, whilst a powerful, rough-haired, surly looking dog followed close at his heels; in short, he would have been taken, at nineteen places out of twenty, for a young farmer, or a farmer's son, travelling across the country on leisurely business, or pleasure.

Betty, the waiting maid, showed him into a comfortable parlour, and having received his commands which he gave in a kindly and unassuming tone, she soon set before him a jug of ale, some cold meat, and bread and cheese.

At that time the hostel of the Grey Mare was kept by a very worthy couple, in their way, named Jacob and Dorothy Deawkintwig, who, with three children, the maid Betty, and Curry the ostler,—claiming to be an offshoot of the Scotch Curries—formed the family group at that well known inn.

The idea resulting from a glance at the person of our host was far different from that conveyed by his name; for, whilst the term Deawkintwig conveys the notion of a slender drooping branch, the person of Jacob presented that strength of body and limb, and height of stature, which are generally found in representations of our old English yeomen. True, he was of quiet demeanour, and almost of child-like simplicity; still he was as fearless as he was simple and powerful; probably nothing human was capable of coercively moving him, except the voice of his wife, and when that broke upon his ear, either in tone of request or command—and the latter was far the most prevalent—he would instantly move as if his pulsation was accelerated, and without a why, or a wherefore, straight set about obeying the command. Still he was far from being devoid of plain, strong sense; in some things he was rather shrewd; had a compassionate heart; and, when out of the hearing of his checkmate, he would launch into conversation, or would joke and banter with the company, always having the fair-

ness to receive back, in good humour, principal and
interest of the jokes he gave out. Like a school-boy
escaped from the surveillance of his pedagogue, he
would enjoy the natural buoyancy of his spirits, but
he was unlike most school-boys in other respects, for
Jacob loved, almost adored his ruler, whilst his rever-
ence for her high qualities, and understanding, was
equal to his love. His fatherly feelings were of the
same mould as the husbands; he doated on his children, especially his first-born son, whose cradle he was
rocking when our traveller entered; he would snatch
his children to his heart, and almost smother them
with caresses, and when, as he supposed, no one was
near, he would try to divert them with a nursery
rhyme, or to sing a lullaby; on which latter occasions
he was sure to be heard by all in the house, for he bel-
lowed like a bull, and generally set the infant a crying.

Mrs. Deawkintwig, both in person and character,
presented, in many respects, a strong contrast to her
husband. She was of middle stature; and, whilst he
was as dark as a dunnock, she was of that excessively
fair complexion, which being too delicate to withstand
our feeble sun, frequently breaks into brown blotches,
called fawn-freckles. Her hair was inclining to what
we call red, and was worn in profusion; her expressive
eyes were of a lively grey colour, and either flashed
with anger, or twinkled with expressions of pleasure,
as the case might be. She was of a good form;
incessantly active; with a rather handsome nose,

thin compressed lips, and a general expression of countenance which displayed more of a will and a determination of her own, than of the milder attributes of her sex. In temper indeed, she was hasty and imperious—held her head high in the town, and failed not, whenever an opportunity occurred, to impress her husband with a conviction of her vast understanding, and unapproachable management. From the servants, and all who dependently approached her kitchen, as well as from her husband, she exacted the most implicit obedience, and that once yielded, she also had her blind side; a word of submission, or of flattery, was quite sufficient to ensure from her, forgiveness, or indulgence.

Betty, the maid of all work, was a pretty, cleanly, hard-handed, apple-cheeked lass, from the neighbourhood of Cannock Chase, in Staffordshire. Her dress was generally a printed cotton bed-gown, or short vest; a knot of strong hair behind, and curls before; a twisted necklace of many coloured beads, a striped kirtle of linsey-wolsey, black, knitted hose, and neat clogs, fastened with clasps of brass upon her feet: after dinner, she would, of course, appear in her gingham gown, with long sleeves and flounces, according to the newest fashion; her feet would trip in a pair of smart shoes; and a green calimanco kirtle might be seen below her tucked up skirt.

As for Curry, the ostler, there was nothing whatever remarkable about his person, and the reader may take him in whatever guise his imagination presents him. The only thing worth notice in his history, so far, was the circumstance of his having been disappointed in love. He fell into the company of a very pretty girl, at a neighbouring wakes, and courted her to the verge of matrimony, without either party knowing the others real surname, until the morning when Joseph Curry was asked at church to Catherine Combe; there was a general titter in the congregation, and the girl that day dismissed him, declaring it had never entered her head to become a Curry-Combe.

Jacob was pleasantly, as usefully employed in smoking his pipe and rocking the cradle, where lay his first-born son, crowing and kicking the clothes off his heels, when the mistress of the house made her appearance from up-stairs, where she had been dressing for the day, and taking the child from the cradle, sat down and gave it the breast.

" Was it Mc. Sandy, or Mc. Rabb that came in?" she asked of Betty.

" Neither of them, Mrs." replied the girl; " he's a young man, a traveller, I think, an I've taen him a jug of ale, meat, and bread and cheese."

" What sort of ale?" asked the landlady.

" Best ale," said Betty.

" Then you put a little alegar into the sixpenny, did not you?" interrogated the mistress.

" Yes," said Betty, " I asked him what sort he would like, and he said our best old ale."

" That's a good lass," said the mistress; " has he a horse ? "

" No," said Betty ; " he came on foot; he's only a dog with him."

" You unconscionable slut !" exclaimed the mistress; " how could you think of putting a tramp, and a dog, into a room furnished as yonder is ? the next thing you'll be handing carters through the bar."

" He's a very farrantly lookin young man," said Betty.

" Dont tell me of your farrantlies; I never knew a respectable traveller who didn't ride on something ; " said the dame.

" The Scotchmen sit in that room, an they dont ride," said Betty.

" And what's that to you, hussey, if they do ; arnt they respectable tradesmen, and good customers," replied the mistress; " have you the impudence to compare them with highway tramps, and dog trailers ! marry, come up ! I wish I'd never heard that."

" No, mam; I dont compare them with any one," said the lass, in a humble tone : " no doubt you know better than I do, what tramps are; you've seen the world more than I have ; only the Scotch gentlemen come on foot, the same as this young man did."

" Yes, Betty, but they'r regular customers; they'r known in the country ; and then, they dont sit over ale ; they've a good tea, or a hot supper, and glass it afterwards. And then consider," said the mistress—

"consider what yon room has cost us furnishing. There's the brass fender and the eight days' clock, and mahogany card and dining tables, and prints of the leger, and the great coursing at Waterloo, where my father's sister's son-in-law stands in a corner holding dogs; and there's my likeness in the room, in oil painting, and Jacob's here,—an old sober-sides as he is,—and bran new chairs, and a Turkey carpet that cost no less than thirty shillings, when old Mrs. Dusty's furniture was sold. I say, turn these matters over in your mind, and consider whether if they were yours, you'd put strange footpads into the room. But here, he rings, lass; see what he wants; and if he's done, we'll shift him into the tap at once. Be sharp, will you."

Betty did as she was ordered, and returning into the kitchen with the tray in her hand, proceeded to pour some hot water into a jug.

"What's that for?" demanded the mistress.

"He wants brandy and hot water," said the girl; "and to speak with master."

"Master! what can he want you for, Jacob?" said the mistress, musingly.

"Mayhap it's something about those sheep at we picked up last week," said Jacob.

"Betty!" said the mistress, prompted by female curiosity; "take the child, and I'll go in with the brandy and water myself."

"Hadn't I best take it in?" asked Jacob.

" No ! sit still till I come back; and if he really wants you on business, you can go in then," said the dame, and with that she took up the tray and entered the room.

The stranger was looking at a newspaper; but on seeing the mistress, he courteously accosted her, and said if Mr. Deawkintwig were at hand, he should be happy to have his company over a glass.

" He will attend you directly, sir," replied the good woman, whose austerity,—the moment he spoke,— became changed to a most obliging manner.

" Bless me !" said she, on returning to the kitchen, " yon is a civil and well-behaved young man, to say the least of him. Jacob, you must go to him, he wants you for something : Betty, take your master's glass in. Why you ninnyhammer," she continued, —addressing the patient servitor—" you might have told me at once that yon person was none of your common padding tramps."

" I told you what I thought, mam ; that he was a decent young man, but you chose to think differently, and so you have done best to judge for yourself," said Betty, as she went to attend her master's bell.

After the usual introductions of civility had passed betwixt Mr. Deawkintwig and the stranger, the latter enquired about a farm which he saw was advertised to be let, and which he understood was in that neighbourhood.

Deawkintwig said he knew the farm right well; it

was the property of Sir Thomas Lookout, as indeed, the whole of the manor was; and Daisy-knowe, the farm in question, was as nice a bit of land as any on the estate. The present family and their predecessors, he said, had farmed it, time out of mind, but something had fallen wrong betwixt widow Barnet, and the agent of Sir Thomas; and she being unable to come forward with her rent, was to be sold up the day following, and the farm was to be let. Every one was sorry for the widow, said Jacob.

"Was she much respected then?" asked the stranger.

"Very much," said Deawkintwig; "she is a worthy woman, and has been unfortunate."

"That was a pity," said the stranger.

"First her husband died," said Jacob; "then her eldest son, who was the main stay of the house, died; then her second son went abroad, some said to the East Indies; then her youngest daughter got entangled with a young spark of an officer, whose party was sent out here during the first election. Some said they were married, but however it was, a child increased the family, and added to the old woman's trouble of mind. The girl has scarcely ever been abroad since; she has stopped at home, and has worked like a horse, they say, to keep her old mother's head above water, but all wont do, it seems; and now they will be rooted out of house and harbour."

"I wish," said the traveller, "the poor woman may

have a good sale, and find something over and above paying her rent."

"I wish she may," said Jacob, "for if she doesn't, she will find herself unroofed in her old age, it is to be feared."

"I should like to walk over the place," said the stranger.

"That you may easily do," said Jacob, "it is not more than a mile from hence, and if you dont know the road I'll go with you, if you'll accept of my guidance."

The traveller thanked him, but said the day was too far spent, and he should perhaps come on the morrow to the sale.

Jacob then asked how far the stranger purposed going that evening? and was informed that he intended going as far as Brimbeck, where he had a friend to see.
Jacob said it was good six miles off, and nights came early at that season.

The traveller said he did not think much of walking twice that distance, either by night or day; and after receiving a few directions, he called for the shot, and paid it, and was about to depart, when Jacob noticed his dog which lay on the floor, casting wistful glances at his master. He was a rough, broken haired dog, young and powerful, though not large; as ugly a looking brute as we might meet with in a year's travel, and, as his master said, chiefly remarkable for his ugliness, and a set of fangs more like those of a wolf than of a dog; in confirmation he laid hold of him and showed his teeth.

"What's the price on him?" asked the landlord. "Why its a matter I've never thought about," said the young fellow; "its the first time I've ever had the question put."

"Will he do for a tenter? will he bark at night?" queried the host.

"Well I cannot say much for his barking," said the traveller; "he's chiefly in the other line, I should think."

"What! will he hunt?" asked the landlord, in his wonted simplicity."

"No! no! man," replied the guest, "he's chiefly for getting hold and sticking fast."

"Hum!" ejaculated the landlord, "I wanted a bit of a tenter; but he is as you say, a deawr, sulky lookin' thing: what do yo call him?"

"Murky," said the traveller.

"Murphy! is he Irish then?" asked Jacob.

"Not an atom of Irish has he in his carcase, he's thorough Saxon, and that's something in his favour," said the traveller, in as grave a manner as he could command. "I call him Murky because of his sullen temper."

"Aye! that's right; and he's murky enough by the looks of him," said Jacob.

"Do you fancy him?" asked the owner.

" If he was mine I'd take care of him," said Jacob,
I think he'd suit us.

" Take him then, and behave well to him. I believe
he's an honest brute," said his master; " though I
never found much good in him yet."

Murky was accordingly taken possession of by the
landlord, whilst his late owner started upon his journey, at one of those paces, which appear so easy in a
good pedestrian, and which, without the least hurry
carry him about his five miles an hour.

The road lay for some distance, across enclosures
marked by stone walls, and it became evident to the
traveller, soon after his setting out, that the best indicators of the path, were the gap-steads left in the walls
for a passage: the rock-head of that noted hill, called
Cleawd-rip, also loomed before him on the right;
and with these land-marks, and the host's directions,
he doubted not being able to track the way as readily
as if a forest ranger stepped it before him.

He now leaped a brook, and crept through some
stunted alders, and began to cross a field which appeared to be the last patch of enclosed ground adjoining a common. Briskly and lightly, though he trod,
night he found, was treading faster. Old Cloud-rip
seemed less distinct every time he glanced that way;
wide tree-less slopes, and sweeping vales, were settling
into gloom on his left, whilst before him lay what
appeared to be a wayless, shelterless moor, stretching
far below, and darkening to the horizon.

He had not walked much longer, when he found
there was no track before him. He stopped at once,
and tried to discover a path, but nothing of the kind
was perceivable. He listened; there was no sound
save the sooing of the wind in a solitary tree; no light
above; nothing but a thick rayless air; and not a
gleam below, except one that seemed at great distance,
somewhat on his right. He inclined to blame himself for adventuring forth, that, however, would not avail.
He thought to return, but that was scarcely practicable,
as there was now, not any way-mark, either before or
behind; he therefore resolved to make for the only
object he could perceive, namely, the light before-mentioned. As he proceeded, complete darkness overtook
him, and had he not carried as good a pair of eyes as
ever did night-hunter, he would have had many an
unpleasant flounder into quags and over jutting boul-
ders; but he escaped pretty well considering all circumstances, and after a long and tiresome tramp, he
found himself at the door of an old stone building, like
most of the habitations on the moor-sides of the
county. He looked through the window; a lamp
hung from the ceiling, and a few sparks of fire were in
the grate; before which, sat an old dame whose visage
and manner brought to his mind the stories of Mother
Demdike, and other witches of Lancashire. She was
seated on a low chair rocking a child, which kept
whining in a cradle, whilst she sung the following
words, to an air he had never heard before.

" Bla bla Blacksheep,
Hasto ouny wool ?
Turn ogen, curly yed,
And fillthe poke full.
Sum forthe meastur,
Sum forthe dame,
An sum for that little lad
At lies ibed lame."

He could only see part of the room, but there were evidently other persons within, as shadows occasionally darkened the opposite wall, and the clack of a shuttle was heard.

When he knocked at the door, the old woman gave over croning, and a female of youthful appearance, but of a care-worn and dejected look, opened the door, and bade him step in, which he did. A pale emaciated young fellow sat at a loom, weaving calico. He ceased weaving when the stranger entered, and began to cough in a painful manner, the perspiration standing in drops on his forehead. He looked a wistful and staring look, as gasping for breath, he rested on his loom.

It was a sad looking place, was that cottage, though quite clean in appearance. Another loom, but without work, stood beside a window; not a particle of any thing like food was to be seen; the place felt miserably chill; the air mouldy and stagnant; the walls were oozing wet; the floor black with damp; whilst, as if to make it still more dolesome, the wind was heard at intervals, howling o'er the lumm, and down the cold dark chimney, in tones quite in unison with a place so lorn, and beings so destitute.

"Wot may be your wish, sir?" asked the young woman, in a manner rather polite, as the traveller gazed around, forgetful of himself.

"God help you, poor people," he ejaculated.

The woman looked surprised. The weaver raised his bony, blue-veined hand, and wiping his clammy forehead, said in a humble tone, "thank yo sir, an may God bless yo."

"You are the new overseer, sir, I suppose," said the young woman.

"Oerseer! oerseer!" interrupted the old one, "hooa ever yerd God bless yo, come eawt ov an oerseer's meawth?" and then she began winding again at a furious speed, singing

"Hasto ony wool?
Hasto ony wool?
Fillthe poke full.
Wur I a sheep
Heaw warm cud I sleep."

"I am not an overseer. I almost wish I were, for your sakes," the stranger said, "I am travelling in these parts, and am wishing to get as far as Brimbeck to night, but I fear I am far out of the way."

"Weer didn yo start fro?" asked the weaver.

"I set out last from the inn at Webster-dyke," replied the traveller.

"Then yo are indeed eawt o' yur way," said the weaver.

> "Eawt oth way dusto say?
> Why dus he stray?
> Iv he'll not stop o'whom,
> Hie him away,
> Till he meets dooming day."

sang the old woman again.

The young woman motioned him not to notice her, intimating, what he had begun to suspect, that she was not in her senses.

The weaver dragged himself off his loom, and taking the lamp, hobbled to the door, and pointing across the fold, asked the stranger if he saw a gate? He replied that he did. "Well," continued the man, " yo mun goo throo that, and keep byth wall-side, till yo gett'n toth' top oth' hill, yo'n then yer a roor o' weatur, unless th'clews are up, an mayhap yo may see a leet afore yo; but however, yo mun make forth' weatur, an follo' th' bruck, till yo comn to a brig, an yo mun goo o'er it, an op th' lone till yo comn to some heawses, an th' foke theer win sho yo th' road eend-way."

The stranger thanked him, and remarked that they seemed very poor and destitute. "Poor indeed!" said the man, "but still honest, I hope." "I hope so too," said the traveller. "No bein i' this heawse," continued the man, "has tasted food sin yuster-neet, except th' chylt, an there's no pap for it neaw."

" And how happens it to be so ? " asked the stranger.

" It wud be a weary lung tale," said the man, " to tell it o'; but th' short ont is, at I am ill,—deein i' fact. My wife, at shud weave o' that tother loom, has had no wark a lung time ; th' owd womon, as yo seen, isno her own person ; an wot wi rent, an foyer, an sickness, wee'n bin torn deawn, and conno get op ogen ; we conno even get one meal a day."

" And the overseer, have you not been to him ? "

" Yo may be sure at we han ;" said the man. " He refust to relieve us, an we summunt him, paying th' last farthin at we had forth' summuns ; an th' justices orthert us to attend at th' vestry, which dusno sit till th' next week, an so iv we con live till then, we may happen get summut, an if we dee'n, we shanno want it," said the poor fellow, leaning against the door-post.

" Had I resided permanently in this neighbour-hood," said the stranger, taking out his purse, " I might have rendered you some service, but as my stay is likely to be short, accept that in return for your present services," and he put a broad piece of silver into the man's hand.

" A theawsun, theawsun blessins on yo, kynd gentleman," shouted the poor weaver, as well as his feeble voice enabled him. " I wudha gone wi yo mysel, but yo seen I'm so kilt for my wynt. " Good neet, sur ; good neet," again he shouted. " Good neet, kynd sir, a hunthurt times o'er," said the young woman, who stood at the door with her child in her arms, tears of oy and gratitude glistening in her eyes.

" Didno I tell the at we shud'n ha good luck ; " the young woman said, kissing her child, and shutting the door. " Didno I tell the so, yusterneet, when th' cinder flew eawt oth foyer, an it wur a purse, an this mornin when I don'd me stockin oth left leg furst, an it wur th' wrung side eawt. God bless my little bab ! " she continued, " but it shall ha summut in it pap soon.

" I dunno believe i' sitch yethen nonsense," said the husband ; " it's o the providence ov a good God, an so let us goo deawn on eawr knees an thank him."

That poor and humble couple drew each a seat, and kneeled down before it ; the old woman also ceased winding, and took the whim to join their devotions, in her way. The man poured forth his feelings in terms of the most fervent gratitude. He recounted his unworthiness, and his many acts of sin against God ; he remembered God's great mercies towards himself and his dear family ; how they had been sustained under affliction of body, and tribulation of mind : how amidst all their troubles they had been mindful of another and a better world, where sorrow was unknown, and the weary were at rest ; and he humbly besought God to prepare them for so blessed a change. He next implored blessings on the head of the kind stranger who had been the instrument that night for effecting another of God's merciful interpositions on their behalf. He prayed God to protect their benefactor in the dark shadows of the night ; to be his guide and his supporter under all the circumstances of life ; to return him in safety to his family, to his old father and anxious mother, if he had such, who were perhaps waiting to hear his welcome footsteps at the door : to bless all belonging to the stranger, however they were related ; and finally he prayed God to remember him on that great day, when he should say, " Come ye blessed, for I was hungry, and ye gave me meat."

During this affecting act of heartfelt devotion, the sobs of the wife prevented her utterance, except the broken ejaculations, " Thank God! thank God! Lord, accept our prayers! God bless him! God bless him! God save him!"

The old woman also occasionally prayed, and as they were accustomed to her ways, there was no interruption, nor breach of gravity. Her constant expressions were, " Bless the Lord, O my soul! and let all that is within me bless his holy name. Bless the Lord, Oh my soul! Jack, set th' porritch on; Bless the Lord! Jack, Jack, fotch sum meal, mon. Bless the Lord! an wod-cakes too; an mowffens too, mon; an potatus too; there's curn i' Egypt yet. Eh; bless the Lord! Jack, bless the Lord."

The husband and wife arose from their knees, and met each others looks with moistened eyes and tranquil hearts. The old woman was despatched to the yard, to bring in a turf or two, and the last piece of coal : whilst the wife, on the certainty of being able to repay, hurried off to the nearest house, about a half a mile distant, to borrow a piggin of meal, and an oat-cake, if they had any.

The fire was quickly blazing; water was shortly afterwards boiling in a pan; the wife, who was not long absent, returned with meal and bread; and what was more, a little treacle; a good warm dish of porridge was soon smoking on the table, and that grateful family, after asking a blessing, partook, were satisfied, and returned thanks.

TO THE EDITOR OF THE PRECURSOR OF UNITY. *

REVD. AND DEAR SIR,

I am greatly obliged by your sending to me the two first numbers of your publication, " The Precursor of Unity," both of which numbers I have read with much pleasure; though, I must confess, I have no very strong hopes of your being able to carry out the plan of association which you propose. Men's habits, thoughts, feelings, wants, and dispositions are so various, that I hardly think it possible for any human means, so far to divest them of their individuality, as to make them work permanently for one common object only. The spectacle of bees working in a hive certainly presents to our contemplation a striking and persuasive example; but after all, bees will be bees, and men will remain men, ever diversified.

---

* " A Monthly Magazine for the Many, illustrative of the System of Association upon Christian Principles, for the production and distribution of Wealth, and the Physical, Mental, and Spiritual improvement of Mankind."
Metcalf, Grocer's Hall Court, Poultry.

Who knows also, but it may be an exactitude in the physical formation of bees, producing an exactitude of wants, and, consequently, of habits, which compels them to labour in the harmony which they do? Men, we know, are ever varying, both internally and externally. In some a peg appears to be too far driven, with others it is loose, and they are ricketty; with one a cord is tightly strung, with another it is too tight, and they are fearfully energetic; with another it is slack, and he is feeble. One man has a dry, hot skin, a hot breath, and his blood goes along his veins at a ramping gallop. That man, whether he think or not, must act,—he cannot be still; another perspires when he exercises, and he will be cool in action; his breath does not scorch his tongue, and his blood moves with a tranquil force; gush,—gush,—no hurry, no impetuosity is there, no palpitation; that man shall think, whether he act or not,—he cannot help thinking. So we humans, for some wise purpose of providence, no doubt, vary continually, and shall do so I believe, as long as our race exists. Now, such men, you cannot, by any means of which I have heard, induce constantly to draw all one way at one time; the wants of their bodies, and the desires of their souls continually prompt them to individual action. The wish for final salvation is perhaps as universal as any one wish of the human race, yet, how various are the modes for obtaining it. The desire to be united with the happy in a future state, pervades all our hearts, yet how few of our fellow-beings are there with whom we choose to associate in our search for eternal happiness? Money again, we nearly all want, but we dont go in flocks to seek it, in whole nations, as rooks go to their food; we disperse, and break into little companies or parties, or act individually, and the means we make use of to obtain our idol, are as various as are our dispositions.

Thus you see, sir, I doubt, whether men,—that is, any considerable number of them,—ever can be brought to act permanently, and voluntarily for one common object irrespective of self. I should, I must confess, like much to see the plan of the bees tried. I should like to watch the progress of an experiment with a thousand or two of our young bairns, rescued from the contamination of the world, and trained up, body and mind, to every noble and christian purpose. I should like to watch the budding of that orchard bloom: to behold the fruit of that harvest. Possibly something like an unity of disposition, and of action for good, might be thereby produced; but, though I wish it might, I doubt whether it ever can be produced by experimenting on grown persons, and fixed habits.

But, there is one part of your plan which was tried and found to answer nearly two thousand years ago, and consequently, there cannot be any doubt as to its answering now, if fairly tested. Jesus Christ tried it, I think, when he gave sight to the blind, and healed the lame, and fed the hungry, and comforted the afflicted, and I have not found any account of His

having failed, in any one case. You do well, therefore, to copy His patent, which is enrolled in heaven's
chancery, though almost forgotten on earth. You cant
do better than stick to His plan, which like all good
plans, begins with the beginning, and ends with the end.
In heaven and on earth, divine wisdom works in one
unvarying way; and true christianity is only an ex-
emplification of that divine wisdom. Jesus Christ,
therefore knew where to begin, and where to end. He
first shewed mercy to the bodies of sinners, and their
souls yearned towards him, even as at this day they
would do, were a great king-hearted benefactor to appear
amongst them, and feed the hungry, clothe the naked,
and comfort the afflicted, as Christ did.

But, the christianity of our days, is I fear, too
etherealized, too intangible for the requirements of
mankind. We may climb to the top of Mont-blanc,
but we cannot remain there, you know: the air is too
attenuated for our bodily life; we must have something
of more substance to breathe, or we die. Even so is
our modern christianity : it is far too high-flighted for
our common comprehensions; it is so fine-spun, that
we cant lay hold of it, and feel it, and appropriate it,
and keep it, and love it: it escapes us, whether we will
or no. The body of our christianity—if I may be
allowed the expression—is so slim and unsubstantial,
that the soul dies in it, for the want of earthly, as well
as heavenly warmth : it is all faith ! faith ! faith ! our
ministers fogetting, or nearly so, that faith without

works is dead: forgetting that, "it is not he who saith, Lord! Lord! but he that doeth the will of my Father which is in heaven;" forgetting, that of faith, hope and charity—the greatest is charity: forgetting that Dives,—whatever faith he had,—was damned for his want of works; forgetting that the first thing Christ prayed for, was bread; and that the last thing he blessed on earth, was that same essential body-sustainer, and soul comforter.

You do well therefore, to look first to the bodily wants of your fellow-creatures; you begin at the right end, and depend upon it their hearts, their affections, will not be far astray from you. What more touching; what more ennobling than gratitude? The heart feels an impulse it perhaps never felt before; it awakes to a new life of pleasure; envy and hatred no longer rankle there; but attachment, and devotedness occupy the place which those former baneful passions once held. Oh! noblest on earth is he who creates gratitude in darkened, and obdurate, and trodden down, and outcast souls; and noble in heaven will he be, when Christ says, "Come ye, unto everlasting rest."

I am, Revd. and Dear Sir,

Yours most truly,

SAMUEL BAMFORD.

WALKS AMONGST THE WORKERS.

No. II.

OLDHAM.

In attempting to describe the actual condition of the labouring classes of this township, I feel that I am entering on a task with still fewer of gratifying subjects in its detail than the one I last performed. Here must be left behind the open fields, the sunny hill sides, the garden plots with their stray flowers; the clear springs, rilling by hedges and down rush-crofts, and shorn pastures, are no longer to be noticed; but, instead of them, we see a multitude of human dwellings crowded round huge factories, whose high taper funnels vomit clouds of darkening smoke. These objects, as we approach them from the west, occupy the slope of a rather steep hill, and the town, lapping over its back, as it were, descends on the other side, and spreads towards the Yorkshire borders at Water Head and Sholver Moor. On the saddle of the hill, if we may so term it, rises the lofty tower of a very handsome church; at the bottom of the hill, on the other side, another church tower, of less elegant proportions, is seen; and on the slope of the elevation, looking towards the south, and a little to the east, stands a noble building, turretted and pinnacled in the Gothic style; this is the munificent endowment called the Blue Coat School, of which the towns-people are justly proud; but both it and the churches, though of a ten years' standing only, are as venerably sombre a hue as if they had stood during centuries. Such is a rude sketch of the appearance of the town as we approach it from Westwood; an appearance by no means so inviting as we shall find the place to be after a little intercourse with its hospitable and warm-hearted inhabitants.

On seeking information in quarters entirely worthy of confidence, I found that the number of inhabitants of the township was, on the completion of the census, forty-two thousand five hundred and ninety-three, viz: twenty thousand six hundred and ninety-one males, and twenty-one thousand nine hundred and two females; that the number of inhabited houses was seven thousand nine hundred and eighty-two; of the uninhabited, one thousand one hundred and six; of houses in building, fifty-two; of mills, fifty-seven; and of mills unoccupied, formerly employing about one thousand hands,—six; that seven mills were working short time, or about five days a week each; that the number of spinners in work was supposed to be about one thousand two hundred; the number out of work, six hundred; and the number who had recently emigrated to foreign parts, or were going about seeking work near home, was supposed to be from three to four hundred; that the number of card-room hands was about five thousand five hundred; of piecers, three thousand two hundred; of power-loom weavers, two thousand five hundred; of hatters, three thousand; of colliers, one thousand three hundred; and unemployed of all trades, about four thousand; that the average earnings of spinners in full work, would be eighteen shillings per week; of card-room hands, six shillings; of piecers, six shillings; of power-loom weavers with two looms, nine shillings; of the same with four looms, thirteen shillings; of hand-loom weavers, (there being however very few in the township), six shillings; of hatters, eighteen shillings; of colliers, sixteen shillings; of shuttle-makers, twenty shillings; of cloggers, twenty-four shillings; of tin-plate workers, twenty-four shillings; of blacksmiths, twenty-four shillings; and of sawyers, two pounds. The sawyers in the employ of one master had just turned out, because he refused to permit men from another yard to come upon his premises during working hours. The whole of the above wages are supposed to require full work to earn them. The number of families relieved from the poors' rate was six hundred and five, or about three thousand and twenty-five individuals, and the amount paid to the poor weekly, in money only, was ninety-five pounds.

The duties of collectors of rates, or of rents, were described as being most irksome. One collector said he never knew any thing like the present state of things before, and he had been in office fifteen or sixteen years. A county rate of seven hundred pounds should have been paid that week, but the money could not be raised, and the overseer had to ask for a few days extra to obtain it; and it was only three months since a similar rate of between five and six hundred pounds was paid. Poverty was increasing on all hands, and the people were getting into a worse condition every week. A collector of rents said people were crowding by two and three families into one house; they could not pay rents for entire houses, and nearly all the workers, who could raise money enough, were leaving the country. These representations were corroberated in many points by other persons with whom I conversed. A master hatter said the hatting branch was dull, but the bonnet trade was rather brisk, and most of the hands now employed were working on that article. A considerable number of men who were engaged in the late turn-out were, he said, still unemployed, and would probably so remain for some time; the masters had got fresh hands, and they would not now receive the old ones; with them they could do no good. This gentleman, however gave a different statement as to their earnings from the one previously set down, he said, body makers when in full employ would earn, at present prices, their thirty shillings a week;

E

roughers would earn the same, and finishers would get from thirty shillings to fifty shillings a week.

Of the state of other employments, some notion may be formed from the following facts which I learned at the several places to which they refer. At a certain millwright's shop, where from twenty to twenty-five hands used to be employed, only one hand was employed now. Shuttle making was stated to be in a bad way; the prices of shuttles had greatly depreciated; and when manufacturers were asked for orders, they said they durst not give any. The leather trade was never worse; the sale of bespoken shoes was dropping off very fast, and working people wore little else save clogs. Shoes were commonly sold on credit, to be paid for by instalments at the pay-day. Some of the shoe dealers went round to collect their weekly payments—a practice which was not known until of late. The clogging business, in consequence of so many being worn, was rather better than had been expected. The strap-leather business had been for some months much duller than previously; the manufacturers kept working their old straps as long as they possibly could, and would not replace them, or any other article, so long as it could be used. Iron founders had very little to do; the men's wages had not been reduced, but many of them were out of employ, and others working short time. In one foundry, where ten moulders were a short time since employed, only one man and a boy were now at work. Machine makers were represented

as not having more than half of the hands employed
which they had two years since; one concern is still
worse, having only three at work instead of ninety,
and an engine master who formerly employed sixteen
men, had now only one apprentice on the premises.
Reed makers, picker makers, rope and band twiners,
and bobbin turners, were partaking the general difficulty of the times, whilst brick making was not more
than half of what it was last season; many hands in
this branch had sailed for America; numbers of colliers had done the same, and these departures accounted, in some degree, for the empty houses so often
visible. Seminaries for the instruction of youth and
children had, in some instances, become nearly de-
serted—one teacher, who lately had a hundred scholars,
had not now more than twenty; and another, who
should have been earning his two hundred pounds per
annum, was getting only after the rate of twenty pounds;
all schools were more or less affected by the bad times.
Pawnbrokers were crowded up with articles pledged by
the poor; such quantities had never been taken in before in the same space of time. Much of their best
clothes and bedding had been deposited long ago, and
now they were in the habit of bringing their meaner
parts of dress for a little present aid. Handkerchiefs,
caps, pinafores, and aprons, they would now pledge
for a sixpence or a shilling " to carry on with," until
something else occurred to sustain them for a few days,
after which their bits of clothing would again be ten-

dered until nothing else was left to dispose of. As no
evil is entirely without some good, it may be stated
that the number of beer-shops is weekly decreasing,
and that a person who, a short time since, could have
counted six of those noisome dens, the "hush shops,"
can now only count one from the same place. A shopkeeper in a large way said, " he now sold as great a
weight of tea and sugar in one and two pennyworths, as
he some years since sold weight of flour in two and three
pound lots." Nearly all his groceries were sold in such
small quantities to the working people, and they seldom asked for more than would just suffice for the meal
they were about to prepare. Flour was selling at from
two shillings and fourpence, to two shillings and sixpence per dozen; meal, at one shilling and sixpence;
bacon, at eight-pence the ℔.; cheese, at seven-pence
to eight-pence the ℔.; malt, at one shilling and eleven-
pence to two shillings per peck ; hops, at one shilling to
one shilling and fourpence the ℔.; and butchers' meat,
at seven-pence to eight-pence the ℔. Some of the
manufacturers, particularly in the "above town" district, were connected with provision shops, and expected
their workpeople to purchase at such shops. The
system of letting houses to the hands, whether they
wanted them or not, was in some instances acted upon
by employers, who also took care to set the rents pretty
high.

The dwellings of the working classes I observed to
be generally very clean; much more so than I had

known them to be twenty- years ago. A great improvement was perceptible in Oldham, in this respect; and now, I am persuaded they will bear comparison, by whole street rows, to those of any houses in the county. The women and children were cleanly attired, and seemed quite as healthy as other town populations, and the men's shirt collars and outer clothes were in a condition which entirely forbade the notion of their having sluttish wives at home. It was evident that the poor people, though sorely pressed, were struggling nobly with their adverse circumstances—that they were fighting with a stout heart, and would not descend to rags and squalor, however they might suffer from toil and hunger. A spirit of honest manly and womanly pride had come over them, and however poor their condition might be, but little of raggedness and filth was seen amongst them. Even the aged and the trembling, and the destitute who stood in the public office waiting for parochial relief, seemed to have put on their best attire to come before their guardians, and their fellows in misfortune.

The health of the factory workers appeared to be as good as that of the general run of operatives similarly employed. Some of the young people in the carding-rooms seemed to suffer from the close air of the place, as was evinced by their sallow complexion and the hoarseness of their voices; but in other parts of the factories, in the cooler and loftier weaving shops, I found a fair proportion of as good-looking youths, and of married persons, as would be met with in one spot, in the country—they were healthy, and really well-dressed in every respect. I remarked this particularly at a shop at Lyon Mill, where three hundred looms were in motion in one room, and at another at Bank-top Mill, near Clarksfield, where perhaps one hundred and fifty looms were at work.

Such are the facts and observations which I now lay before the reader. I present them without comment, and with but little arrangement, lest it might be said that I am directing them to foregone conclusions, with which, however, I have nothing to do. But it should be remarked, that the factory operatives may be classed under three distinct heads, viz., those who are in full employ, and are, consequently, in comfortable circumstances,—those who are only partially employed, and are not so well off as the former,—and those who are destitute of employ, and are, therefore, in distress. The first class consists chiefly of young persons, of both sexes, who support themselves, and contribute also towards the support of other members of their families, where such aid is required, and of young married persons in the prime of life; the second is composed of persons whose strength and activity are on the wane, but whose good character retains them in occasional notice and attendance about the mills; and to the third class belong the sick, the crippled, the aged, and the disorderly, the latter being kept out of the works lest their example should contaminate others. It may also be added, that the second class is receiving frequent augmentations in consequence of the introduction of improved machinery, such as the coupling of large mules or spinning frames, and the practice, (now becoming very common,) of employing self-acting mules, which perform an increased quantity of labour, at much less expense, and in less time than manual labour can perform it.

ROBERT, THE WAITER.

I respected Robert, the waiter at Spooner's well known chop-house, and the more so, because of a little trait of benevolence in which I knew he was engaged.

An elderly person of gentlemanly appearance had been in the habit during several years, of regularly taking his dinner and wine at the place, Robert generally attending on him. At length, after one of the money panics, the gentleman dropped his wine and took beer; and some time after that he ceased taking beer, and asked for water.

At all times he was distant and taciturn, and now more so than before, though he seemed grateful for any little extra attentions that were paid to him.

It was not long ere the quality of his dinners underwent a change; from the rarest and most costly dishes the place afforded, he had now come down to plain beef or mutton; next to half a plate, and at length that was substituted by a small plate of soup and bread.

For a long time his apparel betrayed no change of circumstances. His coat was still fresh and of the newest cut, his hat retained its gloss, his hair was still powdered, his watch guard and rings of gold were still displayed, and his neck-kerchief and linen were of the clearest white, and most neatly plaited. But one by one these exteriors of ease and competence disappeared. His coat became thread-bare, his hat denuded of its beaver, his trinkets were not seen, his neck-kerchief was replaced by a faded stock, and his linen, though clean, was evidently far worn, the wrist band had lost its buttons, and the collar was loose from the gatherings. Still he maintained his distant self respect; and when others were present, he took his soup leisurely, and with the affected indifference of a well fed person; but when alone, he was observed to devour it; and there could no longer be a doubt that he was suffering from hunger. At length he began to miss coming to the place for a day or two at once, and then he would step in on the second or third day and have his small plate of soup. His nose became sharp and pinched, his cheek bones protruded, his eyes sunken and staring from their orbits; his lips hollow, and his look earnest and cadaverous. He next gave over coming at all, but at dinner-hour he might be seen, sometimes shivering near the spout, and at other times pacing slowly past the door, when he would look in, stop a moment, as if to inhale the savoury fumes and then walk away.

" I'm sure the old gentleman could like an invitation to dinner," said the carver, as he stood cutting up, " But these are no times for charity, except at home, and there are very good accommodations for such like in the workhouse."

Robert heard these remarks, but he took his tray and said nothing.

There was a young man dining in the room, whom Robert had known before he came to the town, and he asked the young man's permission to invite a gentleman in reduced circumstances to a little dinner, in his name, which the young man instantly acceded to. Robert accordingly stepped out, and told the old gentleman, that a gentleman within wished to speak with him.

The old man appeared taken by surprise, he looked enquiringly, as if he suspected more than met his ear, and then, with his habitual politeness he acceded, and followed the waiter.

The young man, who had got the cue, intimated that they could speak of business after dinner, and pressed the old gentleman, meantime, to partake a trifle of something. The latter acceded with evident satisfaction, and after they had despatched their meal, the young man pretended to recollect an urgent appointment, said he should be glad to see his guest on another day, and departed. The old gentleman now strongly suspected what was really the case,—that he had been invited for the purpose of giving him a dinner, without hurting his self-respect, and he felt grateful both for the act and the motive. He went a second time, and continued to dine there during the greater part of two months, Robert the waiter supplying the funds, and his friend keeping the secret.

At last the old gentleman ceased coming, and soon after the young man received a note requesting his attendance at the Royal Hotel. He went there; it was dinner-hour, a choice repast was set out, and as he stood wondering what all this could mean, his old friend of the chop-house entered, and shaking him cordially by the hand, expressed his gratitude in the warmest terms, and begged to have the pleasure of his company to dinner.

They dined, of course, and whilst taking wine afterwards, the old gentleman gave his friend to know that he had come into the possession of an independence; and expressed a determination to make an ample return for the kindness experienced at his hands.

The young man, with a rare virtue above temptation, declared the truth; how Robert the waiter had broached the plan to him, and afterwards continued to pay for the refreshments, his own means, as he said, and truly, being too limited to allow of his being generous.

Robert, the waiter, is now a gentleman by property, as he was before by the ennobling virtues of humanity and generosity. The old gentleman, besides giving him a fortune, has made him into his heir, and is spending the evening of his days, at a pleasant little box in the country, carefully and tenderly nursed by Robert and his amiable wife, and amused by their prattling children.

Robert's friend was not forgotten; he soon after went into business on his own account, and the integrity with which he set out, has marked the whole of his career. He has consequently escaped the speculations and wrecks of the times, and bids fair for becoming one of the leading characters on change.

TOM WOODFORD.

I knew Tom Woodford well; he was a decent, hard-working, unpretending young fellow. He once applied for a situation in a Manchester warehouse; it was a subordinate place to be sure, but he had been out of employ long, and neither he, nor his poor old father had latterly had what they should have had, so Tom would put up with any thing for the old man's sake.

" What religion are you of ? " asked the master.

Tom, who was expecting being asked about goods, warehouse work, or book-keeping, was rather taken unaware by this interrogation, but replied, " that his religion was to do as much good as he could, and as little harm."

" Very well ! " said the master, " I like thy reply ; there is only thee and another young man for the place, and if I dont engage him I'll take thee; call again next saturday, and thou shall have a final answer."

Tom called again, but the place was engaged ; the

other young man was busy packing up pieces. " I heard a very good account of thee," said the master, " but on the whole I preferred him; he goes to the same place of worship that I do."

Tom went home in a thoughtful mood, to his old father, and pulling out a penny roll, and a little cheese which he had bought with his last two-pence, he laid them on the table. " Take some," said the old man; No, father," said Tom, " I have been with a friend to-night, and have brought that for you; eat it." The old man eat voraciously whilst it lasted; he eat it all, and Tom went to bed without having broken his fast that day.

It was on one of the next nights of winter, when a cry of fire was heard along the streets, and Tom Woodford was soon at the place. The flames had spread through nearly the whole of the inside of the building; the engines seemed to play in vain, and a few daring fellows only remained throwing out burning pieces. Suddenly one was seen standing on a window sill, with the books under his arm, which had been given up as consumed. " Tom Woodford! Tom Woodford!" exclaimed a number of voices, " he'll be lost, he'll be lost!" " Tom, Tom, come down!" shouted his old grey-headed father, wildly rushing through the crowd. Tom seemed to hear the voice, and waved his hand as if in token; at that moment the roof fell in with a dreadful crash, carrying down the half-burnt floors; a red glaring blaze rose to the heavens, and there was a general cry of " poor fellow ! poor brave lad ! "

Tom was shortly after pulled out of one of the cellars, the books still in his arms; one thigh broken; his hair was burned off his head; and his eyes were scorched blind in their sockets. He was taken to the infirmary, and every possible assistance was rendered, but he died in a few days.

The warehouse was the one at which he had applied for a situation'; the firm set up in another building, and they discharged the warehouseman whom they had preferred to Tom, he having remained during the fire, at a safe distance, uttering ejaculations, and imploring divine interposition.

" We do not disapprove of your religious feelings," said the master, " they are at all times proper, but on this occasion you should have prayed working."

About three weeks afterwards, a bier with a coffin upon it, covered by a humble grey pall, borne by six lowly looking men, with threadbare cloaks and faded scarfs, and followed by an official looking personage, went slowly through the street. Some one had the curiosity to ask, " whose funeral is that ?" and the answer was, " Tom Woodford's father."

The old man was never well after that dreadful night. He became delirious, and the last words he uttered were, " Tom ! Tom ! come down."

WALKS AMONGST THE WORKERS.

No. III.

HEYWOOD.

HEYWOOD is a large and modern village, in the township of Heap, the parish of Bury, the magisterial division of Middleton, and about eight miles north-west of Manchester. The township is near two miles in length, one and a half in breadth, and comprises about two thousand two hundred and forty statute acres. It is bounded on the north by the township of Birkle-cum-Bamford, on the south by those of Pilsworth and Unsworth, on the west by that of Bury, and on the east by the townships of Castleton and Hopwood. Heywood has but recently come into note as one of the largest and most populous villages in the county of Lancaster; for which advancement it is indebted to the mines of excellent coal in the townships of Bamford and Hopwood, and to its industry in the production of manufactures. Forty-five years ago there was not probably a foundry, a machine-maker's shop, nor a cotton factory in the place—that of Makin mill (commenced by old Sir Robert Peel) excepted.

It was then inhabited by a few hundreds of hand-loom fustian weavers and manufacturers : it has now the appearance of a busy and populous manufacturing town, having several cattle fairs yearly, but no market. The number of houses, according to the last census return, is two thousand nine hundred and fifty-two—viz : occupied, two thousand six hundred and ninety-one ; empty, two hundred and fifty-nine; and in building, two. The number of cotton factories, and of woollen and fulling mills, is, according to the same return, forty-one—of which thirty-one are at present working full time, three are working four days a week, and seven are standing unemployed. The amount of population in the township is fourteen thousand eight hundred and forty-seven—viz : seven thousand and seventy-one males, and seven thousand seven hundred and seventy-six females.

From enquiries and observations made by the writer on the spot, it would seem that the working classes in the township of Heap, and those in the village of Heywood in particular, are by no means in so destitute a condition as the operatives of other districts are currently represented to be. Here (at Heywood) a public officer states, " That the rates are certainly somewhat difficult to collect, but that the poor are not yet in that low, starving condition, of which so much is heard at other places ; that a new rate of one thousand five hundred and fifty-four pounds has been laid, and it must be collected by the twenty-fifth of March, 1842 ;

that there are no arrears of rate, for the churchwardens and head overseers will not allow a new rate until the old one has been collected or accounted for; and that about seventy persons only have been summoned for rates during the year, and those were cases arising as much from a spirit of reluctance, as inability to pay." The system of the collector of rates in this township deserves notice, and is worthy of imitation. He calls on the working people on Saturdays after they have received their wages, and before they are entirely disbursed; and he generally receives a trifle, more or less, towards keeping them clear in the book. Shopkeepers and other tradesmen he makes a point to call upon on Tuesdays; and the large ratepayers, the manufacturers and landowners, on Wednesdays. And thus, by an undeviating method, affording the poor opportunities to pay when they have money, he keeps his book clear; and at the close of the year he can say, " There are no arrears of rates."

Most of the manufacturers pay their workpeople fortnightly; one or two pay weekly; and at one mill it is found more convenient to pay for the work on the same day on which it is finished. From the information the writer received, he would suppose the average earnings of card-room hands to be seven shillings weekly; those of piecers, at six to eight shillings; those of weavers, from nine to twelve shillings, according to their number of looms; and those of spinners, at twenty shillings clear; supposing all to be working full time.   One manufacturer, a most respectable referee, supposed the average weekly earnings of the whole of his hands (and he employed eight hundred) one with another, would be twelve shillings a week; at a rough guess he calculated that the average weekly earnings of the factory population of the township, when in work, would be about ten shillings per head per week; but if we suppose nine shillings, we shall be pretty safely within the mark.

It is only recently that the three mills working short time have commenced doing so.   One of them is in the twist line only, and another is in the manufacture of light cloths.   It is probable that three out of every four lbs. of cotton brought to Heywood are made into fustians, which is a branch of manufacture which has felt less of the depression of trade, than perhaps has any other of the cotton fabric; three-fourths of the hands have, therefore, with slight interruptions, been kept at work, and, as was observed by one party, " so long as a family are in employment they know little of distress."   " The workers," observed the same person, " have not yet begun to feel the pressure of actual distress; the shopkeepers and others of the middle class are more embarrassed; and next to them are the manufacturers, whose credit and capital are at stake; many of these classes are in reality distressed; for though they do not experience want of necessaries, they feel distressed by the badness of trade, and the consequent involvement of their money transactions.

Most of the shopkeepers, it was stated, sold their goods on credit, and took pay by instalments; when a family was thrown out of employment, or partially so, the payments would cease, unless work was again obtained speedily. In that case the debt would be worth very little, factory hands being in the habit of removing to other places, and their habitations being rarely so well furnished as those of operatives working at their own houses."

A person, well acquainted with the condition of the operatives, informed the writer, that many of those out of work were in a most distressed condition, both as it regarded their food, clothing, and bedding; and, that so numerous were the applications for relief at the residence of a wealthy and benevolent tradesman, that the lady of the house was quite at a loss how to comply with their solicitations. A schoolmaster said his receipts this year had been so much as fifteen shil'ings per week less than the year previous. He described the condition of his neighbours as very bad; he had from sixty to seventy very fine children of both sexes in the school, all of whom were no less than *well* dressed, very cleanly in their apparel, and, with one or two exceptions, healthy in their looks; and, without doubt, well fed. On this being remarked, he said they were mostly the children of persons above the common level of working men, such as book-keepers, over-lookers, and the better sort of workmen. The children of another school were, however, going to dinner soon after, and the writer observed that they were about as good-looking as those he had just left.

The habitations of the factory hands were of a slighter build than those which the writer had noticed at Crompton and Oldham; they seemed to have been run up quickly, and for present need almost; they were not in general so well finished in the interior. In one of these houses a working family were just finishing their dinner of butcher's meat and potatoes. They all seemed to be in good health, well clothed, and cleanly, and two good-looking young girls were in robust health. The floors were clean, the walls white, and the housewife had gotten her week's clothes well washed and hung to dry on lines across the house. They gave the same account of the condition of the which unemployed, as well as the short-time workers, others had done, saying they were very much distressed, and many families were actually starving. Their own condition, they candidly acknowledged, was much better. They were five of a family, and three were workers. One of the daughters earned eight shillings a week at a carding frame, and another daughter and the father, got seven shillings a week each at steam weaving. Out of this they paid one shilling and a penny per week for coal, two shillings and sixpence for rent; and soap and candles could not be less than nine-pence per week, so they would have four shillings and fourpence to pay for these extras, leaving them seventeen shillings and eight-pence for meat and clothing. This may be considered a fair account so far as they were concerned; but it must be remarked that the two weavers were working short time.

Perhaps the best opportunity of noticing a mixed crowd of factory hands is at noon, when they are going from, or returning to, their employ. The latter was the case in the present instance, and the writer does say, that, at Heywood, he was both surprised and pleased on beholding the hands, of all descriptions, going along the main street, in cheerfulness and civility. He recollects a time when such would hardly have been the case. The young lads were, moreover, cleanly and well clad; there was not a ragged jacket in the whole lot, and they all wore good warm wooden clogs. The girls were as well dressed, and as cleanly, or more so, if it were possible. There was not a torn petticoat nor gown to be seen, (for they all wore gowns) nor one dim or sluttish. All were neat and becoming. It was raining smartly at the time, and the girls in consequence, were all covered, either with stout cotton napkins tied round their heads, or with good woollen shawls, or else they carried umbrellas, and not one of hese latter were either broken or shabby. A very pleasing and becoming pride, the pride of decency, appeared to be commonly felt and acted upon by the young people of both sexes. So much for the factory working population.

Blacksmiths were earning twenty-four shillings per week, when at full work, but many were working short time. A master, however, allowed that there were other places at which the smith trade was doing worse. Moulders in iron works were getting their usual wages of thirty shillings a week, when doing full time; mechanics, turners, and filers, would have twenty-four shillings, but all these branches were often on short time. Fustian cutters, of whom a considerable number reside in one part of the village (Goodwin-lane) were all doing very well; many of them would probably earn their fifteen shillings a week regularly, and some of them so much as twenty shillings.

On the whole, we may conclude, that, as at other places, those of the population only are distressed, who are in want of employment, and according to the estimate of an intelligent person, they were here about one-sixth of the whole number. Nor were all such in the extremity of destitution, but some were much better, some much worse off, than were the bulk of those out of employ. Of the number of factory hands there was not any account in the town, and therefore, for the present, the number out of employ, or partially so, can only be approached by a guess, which, in the absence of sufficient data, it were best to decline.

THE TRAVELLER.

CHAPTER II.

"Weer i'th name o' owd Sooti, hasto fund that four legg'd fiend?" said one, of two ill-looking fellows who were carousing in the tap-room of the inn, as the landlord led Murky through, to consign him to the stable.

"I'm lucky, am not I?" said the host.

"Theawrt olis lucky," said the man, drawing his pipe from his mouth, and looking closely at the dog; "hooas stown him for the?"

"He favvors one at went fro Squire Farrinton's o' Leylond; a tramp stoole him, an' they follo'd him into Yorshur, an' gan him three months at Preston," said the other fellow.

"Yon yung gentlemon at's just set off, has made me a present on him," said the landlord. "He seems to think he's good for nowt, but I know whether he is or not; his breed shows that: did'n yo ever see sitch o meawth," he continued, showing the dog's teeth, somewhat carefully.

The first speaker then laid hold of Murky, and patting him, sang :ʼ

> "Neaw my dogg gen thy dogg,
>   I'll bet-te, wot-to will
> At my dogg, nor thy dogg
>   Will sooner hunt, an' kill.
>
> Aye, my dogg's a shy dogg,
>   Whene'er abroad he goes;
> No high-dogg is my dogg,
>   For deawn he lays his nose.
>
> Back thy dogg, gen my dogg,
>   On that I know of him,
> 'At my dogg, for thy dogg,
>   Shall either hunt or swim.
>
> No dry dogg, is my dogg,
>   No weatur doth he fear;
> Nor shy dogg is my dogg,
>   Whene'er the game is near."

" He's a bonny un," said one. " He's a worryer," said the other; "wot yung gentlemon wur it at ganʼ him the ? which road is he gone ?" he asked.

" He's a stranger to me, an' toth' country too, I think," said the landlord; "but he's a gentleman, I'm sure, an' no dogg stealer; he eawt wi' his purse and paid like a king, an' gan meth' dogg beside."

" I dare say he's one o' thoose Lunnuners, at's comn o'er toth' great heawse at Morningaze," said one.

"I dunno kno hooa he is," said the landlord, "nor weer he comes fro."

"Weer wur he gooin to ?" asked the other.

"He sed heer gooin to Brimbeck, an' I sent him th' road o'er th' moor-edge, and byth' cloof, an' byth' Cudless, an' th' Gronny-Cote; he'll have a fine treawnce afore he gets o'erth' Slip-brigg to neet," said the landlord; "but he's a swipper chap, an' seemt to to think nothin' oth' journey."

"Why, he'll ha to goo byth' Warlocks, an byth' Glyemin-side," said one of them.

"That's just the road," said the landlord, as he lead poor Murky off to his place of durance.

"Mun us try eawr luck to-neet ?" said one to the other, when they were alone. "He mun goo o'er th' Teemin," said the other, "an' we con be theer afore him."

"That's the place," said the first, whose name was Blackstrap; "agreed too," said his companion, Nudger, but—in a lower tone—mind te, we'n goo share an' share alike this time; theaw munno doo asto did when theaw tumblt that owd felley with' spade aces, yed furst, froth' top oth' Skrykers."

"Howd the blab-chops," said the other; "an' ifto will jabber like a un-rest, tawk wi' that white woman at theaw sees folloin' the every time theaw comes byth' Brim-weatur. Eh! theaw doekin!"

"Well," said his companion, "that jobs done, an' its o' no use moythurin one's mind obeawt it. I'll never speak obeawt th' owd mon no moor, if theawl not mention th' woman; so cut thee off, eawt at th' front dur, an' I'll go reawnd byth' Gank, an' o'erta the lung afore thur con be ony business dun."

Nudger immediately went out, whilst Blackstrap stopped and smoked out his pipe, and then going into the yard, accosted the landlord, saying he would give him five shillings for the dog if he would keep him till morning.

"I wudno tak twice five," said the host.

"Twice five!" said the man in affected surprise, "theaw mun be jokin. Come, thea'll let me hav him to-morn, an I'll be summut to drink beside."

"He's no common stuff," said the landlord, opening the stable door cautiously, and calling, "heer, Murky! heer!"

Murky did not make his appearance. "Murky, Murky," again called the landlord; "suss, dogg, suss;" and then he looked into the stall where he had tied him up.

"By G—, he's off," he said; "he's gone yed an' tail shoyar away." "He's bitten th' rope i'teaw," said Blackstrap; he's jumpt through th' hay-hole."

"He's a devil," said the landlord; "he's a devil's imp, goo wheer he will: heawever theers one comfort; he cost me nowt."

"That dus mend it, sartinly," said the fellow, "but iv oather me or th' Nudger leetn on him, we'n bring him the back."

" Wheer is owd Nudger ? " asked the landlord.

" Oh, he leaft me," was the reply; " he had to goo obeawt o pig killin', as far asth' Grimdin, an' he sed he cudno com back to-neet, but he'll be heer ith' mornin."

" Curse the dogg," said the landlord, as he went towards the house.

" Aye ! an' I'll say amen to that, iv I leet on him," said the fellow, as he lounged carelessly past the corner of the stable, whilst the landlord went into the house, in no good humour, having a suspicion that Nudger had stolen the dog.

Whilst ascending the hill which had been pointed out to him from the weaver's cottage, the way-farer heard a kind of whine at his side, and his dog Murky leaped up, and licked his hand, and straight went on in his old abstracted way, trotting beside his master. He was at a loss to know how the dog had got away, or whether, as was most probable, his new owner, taking a second thought, had also turned him out as worthless; however, he made the poor brute welcome, patted him on the head, and resolved, as he had evinced attachment, to observe his ways more closely in future.

On gaining the summit of the hill, after leaving the cottage, the stranger stopped and listened; but he heard not any noise of a water-fall, nor was any light visible, save a solitary one which seemed to be on another higher hill at a distance from where he stood, and betwixt which and himself there appeared to be a deep valley. He therefore began to descend, and, at length came to a water, but as it was too broad to leap over, and too still to be shallow, he sought for the bridge which the man had spoken of, and wandered a long time up and down the bank, but could not find any passage. At length he resolved to swim, and was about to put his purpose in execution, when the sound of a foot arrested his attention, and the next moment he was felled to the ground by a blow which rendered him powerless, but not senseless. Trying to recover himself, he rolled over on his back, and the same moment a knee was upon his breast, and a hand on his throat, throttling him with a deadly grasp. He tried to tear the hand away, but could not; "blast the, deliver," said the villain, "or I'll tear the weasand eawt." The young man tried to lock the villain's foot in his, that he might turn him over, but he could not, and he soon found that he had an old wrestler to deal with. The villain did not strike, he was doing his work better, by taking the breath from his victim, who began to dread being throttled till senseless, and then murdered by having his brains kicked out, and he determined for the last resource of a desperate conflict; he felt in his pocket for his knife, when a short growl caught his ear, and his faithful dog seizing the hand which held his master's throat, sent in his teeth until they were heard to craunch upon the bones. At the same time the villain received a well directed blow betwixt the eyes, and his victim locking his legs, rolled him down by his side, and they both sprung to their feet. The traveller, in turn sought to fell the robber with his crabstick, for the conflict had rendered him furious; he aimed a blow at the villain's head, but it struck an arm, and it fell powerless to his side, when, uttering a cry of pain, he turned and fled, followed by Murky, whose sore lacerations evoked sundry curses, as the villain disappeared in the darkness.

"Wots op," demanded a rough voice at the travellers side, as the last scene had just closed. The traveller cast his eye upon him a moment, and sent in a blow which floored the interrogator like a log. "I'm up," he said, "and thou'rt down."

"Hell gripe thee," said the fellow, and coiling like a serpent, he clasped the travellers legs, and he rolled down on the ground.

"Om not alone," said the robber, as he endeavoured to rise uppermost. "I've others at hond."

"So have I," said the young man, "but I can manage thee myself," and rising to his feet, and stepping back, he dealt one of the most satisfactory kicks that ever was heard to sound on the ribs of a scoundrel.

"Nudger! Nudger!" shouted the fellow.

"That's Nudger," said the traveller, giving him a smasher with his fist.

At that moment Murky seized the villain by the thigh, and the fellow crying out "Oh! curse that dogg!" turned like his companion, and disappeared behind a stone wall.

Murky would have followed, but was held by his master, who had some expectations of a combined attack, and felt sure now of thrashing both, if they came together, but they did not return.

He patted his brave dog, who stood panting at his side. His conscience now, more than ever upbraided him for having abandoned so noble a being to strangers : he caressed him again ; called him his true, his priceless friend ; and vowing never more to forsake him, they went side by side along the bank of the stream, until Murky stood still and whined, when his master stooping, saw a tree lying across the water, with a slender hand-rail attached, and judging this to be the promised bridge, he and his faithful companion went over.

THE TRAVELLER.

CHAPTER III.

AT that time there lived near the place, a very worthy man named Christopher Staidley. He occupied a farm under Squire Lookout, as they called him, who was the principal in the great firm of Lookout and Son, India merchants in London. The elder Mr. Lookout, almost constantly resided in the capital; the younger one, who was said to be a little wild, was at present travelling somewhere abroad; and the management of the property was confided to Mr. Reacho'er, a south country attorney, who with his family, lived at the old hall, at Morningaze.

Besides farming, Mr. Staidley was an extensive manufacturer, and employed at his mill, and in the country round, as weavers, about one thousand hands. His conduct to all with whom he had concerns, was such as commanded more than attention and confidence. The rich respected him, because, besides being an agreeable man himself, and well informed, he was as rich as the best of them, gave parties at his house, and was strictly religious, although from certain strong notions of his own, which he followed up, he was hardly liked by the clergy. With him religion was

> " Not a thing of forms and creeds,
> But of good and noble deeds."

The poor loved, almost adored him; for to them he was at all times, a counsellor, a father, and a friend.

He was upwards of fifty years of age, and a bachelor; in stature he was of the middle height; of mild and prepossessing appearance, though of upright and firm bearing; his hair was dark, rather long, and parted above two calm, clear eyes, which seemed to comprehend without questioning; his features were pale, and their expression was one of benign intelligence.

His sister Edda, was considerably younger than him. She had all the intelligence of his look, but with it was mingled a thoughtfulness which seemed to arise from a constant endeavour to regulate emotions which could not be suppressed. A tender, but severe beauty dwelt upon her features, indicating that though mind subdued melancholy, there was still less tolerance of frivolity there. Her eye was darkly clear; her step was still light, her complexion a healthy pale; her hair was long, glossy, luxuriant, and black as night, save a very few silver threads that had begun to appear; in stature she was rather above the common

G

height; her dress was such as might be expected on such a woman, neither oldly fashioned, nor newly fancied; but, without being strikingly singular, it was conducive to health, neatness, and womanly embellishment. Such was Edda Staidley at thirty; what she had been at fifteen, the gifted only may imagine.

A fair being in the fifth year of her age, whom we shall call Lucy, was Miss Staidley's young companion; she was an orphan, as was commonly supposed, on the mother's side at least, and Mr. Staidley had adopted her as his own; not less from a charitable feeling, than with a view to divert his sister from reflections which at that time had impaired her health and threatened her life. Lucy was a blessing in the house of Mr. Staidley; her innocent and affectionate attentions were at all times soothing and agreeable to her benefactors; the sweetness of her disposition made into friends all who approached her, and when she played, as she sometimes would, on the sward before the door, or laded the crystal clear water from the well, her hair all aloose, down to the girdle of her white vest; when at such times she went forth, and the sun looked on her locks of pale gold, she might have been taken for an immortal being, the genius of the place.

An elderly lady, aunt Frances, or anty, as Mr. and Miss Staidley sometimes called her, was also one of the parlour circle. She was their maternal aunt, the widow of a merchant, who having become reduced, died leaving his wife and a daughter a small annuity only to subsist upon. She was of a venerable age, and accomplished manners ; and besides the value of her agreeable conversation, emanating from a mind chastened by adversity, she both gave and derived pleasure from the instructions and accomplishments which she imparted to the lovely orphan. When conversing with the child, tears would often gush into her eyes, and trickle down her cheeks, as if the recurrence of some agonizing reflection harrowed her feelings.

" Why do you weep ? " the child would say, wiping her tears and kissing her cheek. " Why do you weep, my anty, my dear anty ? cease weeping and I will be a good girl, I will indeed ; I will be your own good Lucy."

The old lady would look on her with inexpressible tenderness ; and then rising and hurrying to her chamber, would remain shut up some time, until probably, having sought comfort where alone it can be found, she would at last come forth, serenely thoughtful, and resume her duties.

The other inmates of the house, were a tidy, neat handed servant maid, clad in mob-cap, a striped bedgown, and a linsey-wolsey kirtle ; Robin o' Dolls was cowman and carter on the farm ; a fine Newfoundland dog, and a cat or two, were favourites with the family ; in the yard were a pretty numerous colony of ducks, geese, and fowls, whilst a young donkey, sometimes stolidly grave, anon as playful as a kitten, took a wisp of hay, or a lick, wherever he found them, and made acquaintance of all around.

The house which Mr. Staidley occupied was a good sized, substantial stone building, with square chimnies, steep roofs, and gables, with low, mullioned windows, and porch, as in the olden time. It stood on the top of a pasture, to which a lane, darkened by hazels, white-thorns, and rose-briars, led up a slope on the left. On the east and south of the green knoll, were precipitous dells, in the calm shelter of which the pine and the yew enrobed themselves in their most brilliant green; the ash, elm, and beech were ranged higher on the slopes, whilst the proud oak, emblem of the indomitable, waved above all, battling with the winds, and defying the storms. Comely sprouts, and matted tendrils were the undergrowth of the place, whilst protected by them, grew wild flowers, and scarce herbs, strewn by the hand of nature, and seldom disturbed by the hand of man.

Behind the house, in the nook of a fine meadow, and garlanded with honeysuckles and rose trees, glimmered a little bright well, paven with white stones, from which, a rill trickled over cresses and sweet herbs, until it tumbled into a trout-stream, as yet uncontaminated; and rising again in bubbles like silver pearls, went murmuring away.

On the north and west were rising grounds, covered with rich herbage, where the primrose and the snow-drop would often peep forth at Christmas. The early spring was first to look down there, and the sunbeams so often traversed that spot, and seemed to linger so long, that, from the earliest settlement of our Saxon ancestors, the place had been known by the name of Glyemin-side.

The interior of the dwelling was not less characteristic of the good English taste of the master and mistress, than were the arrangements out of doors. The reader may imagine a number of rather low, but spacious flagged rooms, fitted up in a style more calculated for usefulness than elegance. Every thing, from the floor to the roof, is scrupulously clean, with walls and ceilings of shining white : a gun or two and some spits hang above a massive oaken mantle tree ; a fire of coal and wood, is spurting from a large clean grate ; in the recess of the chimney, some covered mugs, containing cream, are arranged on one side ; in each nook is a spacious oaken chair, one a little modernized, by having a cushion on the seat, and a foot-stool before it. In the window, balsams and myrtle are growing, and in a vase of special form, is a plant, with broad, red-streaked leaves, pearl-shaped, and a long trailing, languid flower, of blood-scarlet, called " Love lies a bleeding." Beneath the window behold a dark oak table, polished like a mirror, with carved oaken chairs to match at each end ; other stout seats, and a long-settle, or oaken couch, are placed at intervals ; a large dining table ; a spacious shelf with earthenware and another stored with pewter utensils as bright as silver, are on one side of the room. In a dry corner are displayed various articles of brass and copper, all very clean; from the joists and rafters above, depends a large flake stored with excellent oat cakes, home-baked; a tub of ripe ale-wort is humming on a stool, whilst the carcase of a fine hog, well-salted, floured, and hung up, has become excellent bacon. A bridle or two, and a couple of saddles, neatly covered from the dust, hang against the wall, and we may perceive by the stirrup that one of them is a lady's saddle; whilst reins, bridles, hedging-bills, mittens, and other articles are variously disposed. In another room shall be seen a piano, a violin, in a green cloth case; some music books; a set of mahogany drawers with an escrutoire; a mirror in an old fashioned frame of gnarled chestnut, or ebony; stout oaken chairs, and other articles to match; here also may be found a book-case, containing the Bible; the Book of Common Prayer; the Whole Duty of Man; Robinson Crusoe; Thomas a Kempis; Henry, Earl of More-land; Milton's Paradise Lost, and Miscellaneous Poems; Shakespeare's Works; the Pilgrim's Progress; Pope's Iliad and Odyssey; Bunyan's Holy War; Culpepper's Herbal; a true History of the Lancashire Witches; Watts' Hymns; a book on the Diseases of Cattle, and many other useful and instructive publications.

The bed-rooms too are furnished after the same fashion; the windows are thrown open, the breeze sweeping freely through; the air perfectly pure; the floors clean swept; the furniture without a particle of dust; whilst the beds, though not of the softest, are covered with milk white sheets; warm woolly blankets; stout woollen rugs in winter, and printed covers, or bleached counterpanes in summer.

Then in the buttery are beef in salt, and pork in pickle; mugs of home-made butter, both fresh and salted down; a cask or two of flour; a fine cheshire cheese; an old ark stored with meal, and a decent stock of soap, candles, and groceries. In the cellars are sundry stone bottles of ale, several sorts of home-made, and some foreign wines and spirits; kept more as cordials, or for a sick neighbour, or a stranger friend than for the use of the family.

Let the reader picture to his mind a house such as has been described, and stored with every thing necessary to plain, homely comfort; that comfort which, in fact, is known only in England; and which English-women alone know how to produce and conserve, and he will have an idea of the interior of Mr. Staidley's house at Glyemin-side.

THE TWO JUDGMENTS.

IN the solitude of the night I had a strange dream, at which my soul was troubled, and filled with fear and awe.

Methought I was in a large open place, where a great multitude of human beings were collected together. And they were divided into the accepted, and the unaccepted; and they were separated by a barrier, on which stood an Angel, whose robe was as white as driven snow; and the outside feathers of his wings were like frosted silver, and those of the underside were like pale gold; and he stood there as a test and a witness of truth; and he kept a record of the proceedings of these children of men, but they knew not that he was there.

And I perceived that the accepted party dwelt in a beautiful country, like a large park, which was laid out in pleasant walks beneath shady trees, and by quiet and retired places, and amongst shrubs ever blooming, and ever in leaf. And splendid palaces were there, furnished with rich carpets, and soft couches, on which

the weary went to repose; and tables were spread for
them, covered with ever delicious viands; and whatever they wished to eat, or to drink, or to clothe themselves with, was straight set before them. And they
formed a most splendid company as ever was seen
under heaven. Noble countenances were there, and
beauteous and majestic forms; and their garments were
of all bright colours and hues; gorgeous tiaras and head-
dresses they wore; and as they moved, their robes
and jewels gleamed with splendour; and they walked
about in the sun-light, all so happy;—and some
danced to music, and some listened to ravishing
strains, and some had fine pictures and statues, and
some were happy in love, and some had beauteous
children, and others took pleasure in splendid chariots,
and in horses and hounds; but all seemed so happy,
like very angels;—and thus they spent their time
within their pleasant enclosure.

And I remarked that three spirits stood within a
gate, which led into the enclosure; and they kept it
that none might pass within but such as were accepted; and I asked the Angel about them, and he said
they were evil ones; and their names were Ignorance,
Pride, and Hypocrisy.

And Ignorance assumed an air of wisdom; and
Pride was robed in a garment of meekness; and Hypocrisy wore the clothes of a saint.

And the Angel waved his hand, and their garments
were turned aside, and their bosoms opened, and I saw

their hearts, all teeming with arrogance and oppression, and avarice, and perfidy, which they hugged inwardly, saying, "No man will know."

And on the outside of the gate at the barrier, stood one keeper only, and the Angel said he was a blessed spirit,—his name was Hope. And a mighty concourse of men, women, and children stood behind him; and they occupied a vast plain, of which there appeared not any end. And their looks were incessantly directed towards the country inside the barrier, and the splendid company there assembled. And the multitude were agitated by a variety of wants and passions, and they were restless as a tossed ocean; some were torn by envy, some by revenge, some uttered curses loud and deep, some brandished weapons, some plotted to force the barrier, and others betrayed them; some advised conciliation, some laboured unceasingly to hoard up wealth, some were a-hungered, some in rags, some had long been houseless, and they stood there, wind and storm-beaten, praying for food and shelter.

And the Angel looked on the multitude of beings with pity; and he straightway waved his wings of glory, and there broke from them a light at which the sun grew pale, and a feeling of divine mercy and charity fell upon the hearts of many of the people inside the enclosure; and they held meetings, and heard sermons, and made collections, for the instruction, and the moral and religious improvement of the great outside multitude: many of them said also, "lest peradventure they break in upon us, all rude and uncivilized as they are, and take from us our houses and lands, and our silver and our gold; and rob us of our enjoyments;" and so they contributed liberally, and sent instructors amongst the people.

And from time to time those amongst the people, who had acquired wealth, by whatever means, knocked at the barrier, and being deemed respectable, were, by the evil ones, admitted to share the joys and splendour of the place.

And mingled with the people, were good men, and self-taught geniuses, who needed not instruction; and attended not, therefore, to the precepts of teachers, but unto those of God only. And from amongst these from time to time, advanced some to the barrier, to see if peradventure, they might be accepted.

And, as I looked, an old man came from the crowd and demanded entrance; and the keepers within asked on what grounds he claimed it; and the blessed spirit of Hope spake for him, and said he was a virtuous man; he had shared his bread with the hungry, and his garments with the naked, he had protected the defenceless, and had shielded the innocent, and had saved life. And Pride asked if he were wealthy? and Hypocrisy if he were of the true faith? and Hope said he was very poor, and the Angel, yearning, said he would be found acceptable of God; and they heard the words of the Angel, but knew not from whence they came. And the keepers, looking at his humble appearance, declared he could not be accounted respectable, and therefore could not be admitted, and they closed the door against him. And certain men and women, of noble carriage, and with shining countenances and apparel, advanced from the crowd within the barrier, and spoke words of comfort to the virtuous man, and stretched forth their arms and embraced him, and gave him of the food and raiment which they had in plenty, and the poor man was very grateful, and he blessed them and their posterity; and then he went his way and died amongst the people, and there was a great mourning for him, and a lamentation; and he was carried to a quiet green field, and there buried; and the people wept upon his grave, calling him, Father! Father!

And soon after another man came from the crowd. He was of mature years; of a thoughtfully placid countenance, and neatly, though humbly attired; and he had books and writings under his arm, at which he kept looking. And Hope said he was a man of learning, but very poor, and the three keepers looked at him, and saw that his apparel was humble; that his feet were scarcely concealed by his shoes; that his features were shrunken and furrowed by want; and that the only jewel he wore, was a plain ring, on which he glanced affectionately. And when they questioned him, he said his life had been spent in endeavouring to benefit and enlighten mankind.

And Ignorance questioned him about air bubbles; and

Pride enquired about his pedigree ? and Hypocrisy asked if he had written sermons ? and he said he had not written any sermons, unless the tenour of his life and of his writings might be considered as such ; and he was adjudged not to be respectable, and was rejected ; and thereupon certain noble-minded men and women advanced from the gay crowd, and spoke kindly to him, and embraced him, and bade him be of good comfort, and they gave to him that which gladdened his heart, and he blessed them, and prayed God to bless them ; and the Angel which stood on the barrier wrote that blessing in his book, and it was not forgotten in heaven.

And in some time a third man came from the crowd to the gate ; his appearance denoted extreme poverty ; he was bent with the weight of years, and his grey hairs scarcely sufficed to covered his forehead ; and he asked not so much to be admitted, as to obtain wherewith to keep his old age from want. And Hope said he was a naturalist, and had spent all the hours he could spare from labour, in collecting and arranging God's wondrous works in the vegetable creation ; and they questioned him about his moral life, and he admitted he had not been altogether blameless ; but he sincerely repented, he said, whatever errors he had committed, and hoped they would be forgiven. And the Angel wrote down those words, and they were not forgotten of God. And the keepers decided that he could not be allowed relief because his life had not been morally pure; and he turned to go away, but certain noble-hearted men and women advanced from the respectable side, and called him back, and covered his grey hairs with a mantle, and spoke kindly to him, and gave him wherewith to make his latter days comfortable; and he blessed them, and the Angel recorded that blessing, and he took down the names of those who did these good things, and they were blessed above the rest of mankind.

And then came one from the crowd, bearing a harp, and his carriage was dignified and respectful; and he put down his harp near the barrier, and leaned upon it, for he seemed weary with long travel, and his grey hairs floated about the strings. And Hope said he was a bard, and the evil ones inside the gate, would not believe that one so homely could be a bard. And he waved his hand for silence, and when the noise had abated, behold a sweet strain was heard from voices inside the barrier; the respectable ones were singing a new song, and that song was his; and the people took it up and shouted his name. Then the evil ones questioned him about his conduct in the world, but they enquired not what had been the conduct of the world towards him; and he turned away indignant, and dashing the tears from his cheek, he took up his harp to depart.

And certain noble-minded men and women called him to the barrier, and embraced him, and consoled him; and they would have given him food and raiment, and silver, and gold; but he would have none of their gifts, because he was not thought worthy to be admitted; and so he blessed them and went his way. And the Angel wrote down all these things, and he shook his wing above the harp, and there awoke a melody such as never on earth had been heard before. And the multitude listened in ecstacy and wonder; and the minstrel knew not whence the music came, save that his harp was vibrating; and looking towards heaven, he said, " Lord, if it be thy will, let my travail now cease ! " and he leaned on his harp, entranced with the wondrous tones. And when the Angel folded his unseen wing, the music ceased, but the bard stood leaning on his harp as if still listening. And they called to him, but he moved not, and they urged him, but he lifted not his head. And certain of the noble-minded came over the barrier, and others advanced from the crowd, and when they tried to arouse him, he was no more. And they mourned over him, calling upon him with endearing words. And they placed him on a bier, and wreathed his bier with garlands, and they bound his brow with tendrils of young wood-bine, and hazel-bloom,—for it was the spring season, —and they decked his harp with the new flowers of the year, and placed it beside him on the bier, one hand resting on its chords; and they carried him on their shoulders to a green sunny bank, where they buried him, and wept over his grave, saying, " Alas ! alas ! that we should live and hear that voice no more ! " and they placed fresh sods above his grave, and planted there a young broom, emblem of his never fading song. And when they returned, a young bard carried his harp tenderly aloft, and the flower wreaths swung upon it, and the Angel waved his wing, and the same sweet tones were heard as before ; and the people stopped and wept, and looked up, saying, " it is he ! it is he ! our beloved one is still abiding with us." And they were comforted.

And after that a man advanced from the crowd bringing with him a machine most wonderful to behold ; he had spent long days and nights of toiling thought in its construction, so that he had wasted his substance, and was now poor and distressed, and he craved wherewith to enable him to complete his machine, that he might obtain his just reward ; and in order to show what the machine would perform, he turned a wheel, and the machine spun out many fine even threads at once, so aptly almost that it seemed as if moving from reason. And the respectable class praised his ingenuity, but they vouchsafed him not any thing ; and the three keepers at the barrier kept it closed ; and certain ignorant ones advanced from the crowd, and threatened the man, and abused him, and broke his machine, so that he was obliged to flee and hide himself, and he did so, and disappeared, and died in obscurity, and left his children in want. And then came another man with a machine almost like the former one, but more complete, and he carded his wool and spun out his threads as had been done before, and he showed the multitudes on both sides, how those threads might be made to yield gold, and they bade him go on, and he spun many threads and exchanged them for gold, so that presently he was clothed in gold. And the people on both sides set up a great shout, saying, "well done! well done!" and the barriers were quickly opened, and the man went within all laden with gold; and the respectables received him with joy and feasting, and he was accepted by nobles, and honoured by princes, and all because he had shown them how to procure gold. And after that I heard a tender, sweet voice singing a mournful air; and behold it was a woman who came forward in face of all the people. A comely woman was she, dark haired and very pale, and her dark locks were beaten by the wind, and a wreath of dying flowers was upon her head; and she moved slowly, bearing in her arms a babe which suckled sleeping at her bosom. And ever and anon as she moved, she turned towards the crowd within the barrier, looking as if she would fain behold some one there, and pouring forth the while, tones that might have moved a heart of stone; and she sung the joys of innocence, and the downfal of virtue, and the wretchedness of guilt, and many hearts were moved, and many were fortified to good intent. And she essayed to pass the barrier, but the keepers prevented her, and called certain stately ladies, who said she was impure, and degraded, and they were surprised at her audacity in attempting to enter there; and she blushed when they mentioned her shame, and tears fell upon her bosom, and bathed the face of her child. And she said she would not have presumed to come had she not known that one whom she loved, the father of her infant was there; and the ladies denied that he was there, and she pointed him out, walking in grandeur with a bevy of the fairest and noblest. And the ladies reproached her, and bade her begone, saying, " she was not a fit associate for any one in that place," and the barrier was closed against her. And she raised her voice and sung a strain of her days of innocence, and her betrayer heard it, and looked, and saw her, but he moved on and disappeared.

And then her heart sank within her, and she turned to go away, but certain noble-minded ladies came down to the barrier, and they spoke consolingly to her, and offered her food, and clothing, and tried to comfort her. And she thanked the noble-minded ladies, and prayed God to bless them, and that none belonging to them might carry a broken heart, but she would none of their gifts, and so, she went slowly away.

And the Angel wrote down those blessings in his book, and they were recorded as blessings in heaven; and the noble-minded ones were blessed. And Hope, the good spirit would have spoken to the woman as she went her way, but she, turning, gazed upon him with an unearthly gaze, and pressing her infant to her bosom, her full heart stopped, and it beat no more.

And the Angel standing upon the barrier, said, " It

is done," and he closed the book wherein he had recorded the actions of the children of men. And he outspread his wings, and there broke from them a light at which the sun grew pale; and looking towards heaven, he said, "Oh Lord! how long shall thy chariot wheels stay?" And then was heard the sound of a mighty trumpet, and a voice proclaiming, "Make straight the way of the Lord!" And all mankind were sorely afraid: they were changed in a moment, in the twinkling of an eye: the corruptible put on incorruption, and the mortal put on immortality. And the Angel again shook out his mighty wings, and all the earth was one intense light, and all heaven one dread blackness; and there came a wind which swept over all the earth, and under all heaven, and it howled till the cries of the myriads were undistinguishable. And above all the tumult was heard the trampling of ten thousand chariots, and the clanguor of far-off music, like that of a mighty host; and the earth trembled and shook like one in fear, and it uprose and downfell as if in agony. The mountains were cast abroad, and the valleys upheaved, and streams were engulphed, and it tossed to and fro, and shrivelled up like a burning scroll. And the heavens came down like a floor over the earth, and the sun was dim, and the moon like horrid blood, and the stars glared, and meteors burned, and comets rushed blighting all the straightened space. And the sound of music, and the clangour of trumpets, approached; and the blackness opened wide, and a space all glorious appeared, and a multitude too bright and terrible to look upon, descended from the heavens, and in the midst of them was the Father of all things, whom none may describe. And a herald cried with a loud voice, "let all the earth be still," and it was so, and there was silence. And the throne of God was pláced amid the glory under heaven, and his Son, the Holy One, stood at his right hand; his crown of thorns was turned into a diadem of unfading gems, and his cruel wounds into marks of honour. And the tears which he had shed on earth, were turned into brilliants which angels wreathed into chaplets wherewith to crown those unto whom their Lord would do honour. And archangel, cherubim, and seraphim stood around the Almighty; and those who had been faithful unto death for truth's sake, were at the foot of God's throne; and those who had been persecuted and despised of men, were there, also; and the living were called to judgment, and the graves gave up their dead, and the ocean was no more, and the depths where lay men's bones moved with the lost ones that were now found. And all souls were gathered before the judgment seat, and there was silence. And an archangel proclaimed with a loud voice, "let the accepted be divided from the unaccepted." And the Angel of truth opened his book of record, wherein the actions of mankind were written. And the accepted were placed at the foot of God's throne, on his right hand, and the unaccepted were placed at the foot of

God's throne on the left. And many who in the flesh were accepted, now stood on the left side; many also of those who in the flesh were unaccepted, now stood on the right; and a halo of glory shone above them, whilst a terrible blackness brooded over the left. And amongst the accepted I beheld the poor virtuous man, who in the flesh was rejected at the barrier, and by his side stood the poor learned man, and the naturalist, and the bard, and the mechanician, who died unknown; and the poor outcast female, who sung her own requiem, stood there with her infant at her breast; and her broken heart was made whole, and all tears were wiped from her eyes. And they all stood beside each other, and they were arrayed in bright apparel, and each was crowned with a diadem of the Lamb of God. And they were all resplendent and meek in their glory. And I beheld the noble-minded men and women, who in the flesh had welcomed the outcast, and comforted the distressed; and they were each arrayed in bright raiments, and chaplets of the Holy One were placed on their brows, and they stood beside those whom they had succoured and comforted on earth, and they were all arrayed in glory, and they bowed before the throne and the Lamb. And behind, and around, and at far distances, were angels and saints of old, and winged seraphs passing to and fro amid the brightness. And amongst the unaccepted stood many who on earth had worn perishable crowns, and many who had led armies to battle, and many who had worn mitres and robes of scarlet, and all those who had taught in temples for lucre, and they were very many. And the three evil spirits, Ignorance, Pride, and Hypocrisy, with all their followers were there, and they looked sorrowful, and sorely afraid. And many, who on earth had amassed wealth, who had laid house to house, and field to field, whose souls had yearned only after gain, were on the left hand; and those who had wallowed in pleasure and luxury were there, and those who had turned a deaf ear to the supplications of mercy were there, and he who had beguiled the innocence of the heart-broken was there, and the fair and noble ones who had entertained him and comforted him in his guilt, were there, and they beheld him now cast down, humbled, and sad. And also the pure and stately dames who had despised and rejected the unfortunate, all stood at the foot of the throne of God on the left hand.

And God, speaking to the Holy One said, " Son, give judgment." And the Saviour took his seat at the right hand of the Most High, and there was silence.

And the Saviour, speaking to those who were on his right hand, said, " Come ye blessed of my Father, inherit the kingdom prepared for you. For I was an hungered, and ye gave me meat; I was thirsty, and ye gave me drink; I was a stranger, and ye led me to your hearths; naked, and ye clothed me; sick, and in prison, and ye consoled me."

And they to whom he spake, answered, " Lord, when saw we thee an hungered, and gave thee meat; or thirsty, and gave thee drink? when saw we thee a stranger, and sheltered thee; or naked, and gave unto thee clothing? or when saw we thee sick, or in prison, and visited thee?"

And the King answered them, saying, " Inasmuch as ye have done it unto one of the least of these my brethren, ye have done it unto me."

And the humble ones; those who had been dispised and rejected in the flesh, lifted up their eyes and said, " Lord! we thank thee."

And then, speaking to those on his left hand, the King said, " Depart from hence, ye accursed, unto a place prepared for evil ones. For I was an hungered, and ye gave me not meat; I was thirsty, and ye gave me not drink; I was a stranger, and ye sheltered me not; naked, and ye clothed me not; sick, and in prison, and ye visited me not."

And they answered him, saying, " Lord! when saw we thee an hungered, or athirst, or a stranger, or naked, or sick, or in prison, and ministered not unto thee?" And they besought him with many cries and supplications, and he answered them, saying, " Verily! verily! I say unto you, that, inasmuch as ye did it not unto one of the least of these my brethren, ye did it not unto me."

And a trumpet sounded, and an Angel proclaimed with a loud voice, " Come ye blessed into everlasting rest, and ye accursed depart into torments."

And one on the left of the throne cried fearfully, " Lord ! Lord ! thou hast forgotten me ! "

And the judge said, " What wouldest thou ? "

And the suppliant said, " I am one of thy saints, and thou hast forgotten me !"

And the Judge said unto the Angel, " What is recorded."

And the Angel read in his book and said, " Lord ! he was holy in the eyes of men, but a vile one in his heart : his sin was spiritual pride."

And the Judge said, " Let him dwell with the hypocrites : he is no saint of mine."

And he was bound hand and foot, and cast into outer darkness.

And another cried fearfully, " Lord ! have I deserved this ? "

And the Judge said, " What pleadest thou ? "

And he said, " Lord ! I gave a thousand pieces of gold to build to thee a temple."

And the Judge said, " My temples are not built with hands ; whence came thy gold ? "

And the Angel opened the book and said, " Lord ! he was unjust in his dealings ; he oppressed the poor, and he wronged the labourer of his hire. He gave the gold to win him a name amongst men, but he turned the humble from his door, and ceased not to oppress in secret."

And the Judge said, " Scourge him, and cast him into outer darkness."

And demons bound him hand and foot, and scourged him, and cast him into outer darkness, to abide.

And another cried, " Lord ! I was absolved of my sins, and died forgiven."

And the Judge said, " Who absolved thee ?"

And the suppliant said, " Thy servant the priest, Lord ! whom thou hast also forgotten, for he is here."

And the Judge said unto the Angel, " What is recorded of these ?"

And the Angel looked and answered, " Lord, he spent his life in riotous living; he was a glutton, a drunkard, and a debauchee. When nature could no longer endure, he sent for a priest, who, in thy name, undertook to remit his sins, and to administer the rites of religion, for which he received twenty pieces of gold, and the sinner died."

And the Judge said, " let the sinner have his reward; and let the priest be bound and scourged, and thrust out to await."

And the sinner was thrust back, and the priest was seized by demons, and bound, and scourged, and cast into outer darkness.

And a fourth cried, " Lord ! have mercy on thy servant."

And the Judge said unto him, " how hast thou served me ?"

And the suppliant answered, " Lord ! I have been very zealous in upholding thy faith. I have confirmed the wavering, I have reclaimed the wanderer from thy fold, I have rebuked the impenitent, and I have silenced the infidel and schismatic."

And the Judge spoke unto the Angel, saying, "What is written of this plainant?"

And the Angel said he was a bigot, and a persecutor of all who differed for conscience sake. His religion was a creed to which he would have all men conform. He terrified the timid, he reclaimed the wanderers by chains and dungeons, he rebuked the impenitent by blows and cruel stripes, and he silenced the infidel and schismatic by torture and death. "See, Lord! here are thy witnesses."

And many there stood, who in the flesh had passed the ordeal of his cruelties, and they testified against him.

And the Judge said, "let the accursed depart." And he was seized, and bound, and scourged; and none had pity.

And another exclaimed, "My Saviour, let the humblest of thy flock approach thee."

And the Judge looking upon him said, "whence comest thou?"

And the suppliant said, "from thy tabernacle, Lord, which I have attended regularly, three times every sabbath during thirty years; my family also went with me," for I said, "as for me and my house, we will serve the Lord."

And the Judge said, "fed'st thou the deserving hungry, or clothedst thou the perishing naked. Yearned thy heart towards the poor and desolate ? "

And the suppliant said, "Lord, I could not give much to the poor ! I gave it to the missions. I administered to the souls of the poor, Lord ! I gave them tracts."

And the Judge, frowning, said unto the Angel, " What is written ? "

And the Angel said he was a rich man, and very pious in the world's way. He was an enemy to sabbath-breakers, yet he went to chapel in his coach, and was attended sumptuously at home. He gave liberally towards the spread of his religion in foreign parts, and especially when there was a great crowd to witness his gifts ; but when besought in private, he gave only books and sermons, saying, " they were the bread of life."

And the Judge said, "let him depart, his place is with the Hypocrites."

And he was bound hand and foot, and thrust into darkness.

And another said, " Lord ! I never did violence for opinion's sake."

And the Judge asked the Angel what was written ?

And the Angel said he was one of those who loitered about the temples, and did mean offices for the priests; his chief business had been to worm into the private life, and undermine the characters of any who were obnoxious to his employers ; those especially who happened to worship at a different shrine. Many, said the Angel, had been injured by his slanders ; some had been destroyed, and but few ever discovered from whence the injuries came.

"Depart thou abhorred!" said the Judge, and he was bound and scourged, and cast out.

And one of the pure matrons approached the throne and prayed for mercy, saying, "she was the mother of a large family, some of whom were then amongst the blessed."

And the Judge asked her if she had shown mercy to any child of man save her own?

And the Angel read from his book, how she met the lost wanderer at the barrier, and how the suppliant, with others, had reviled and rejected her; and he pointed to the blessed one, who stood there in her radiant vesture.

And the Judge said to the suppliant, "go thou unto darkness." And with sorrowful lamentations she departed to her doom.

And ten thousand times ten thousand Angels awoke songs of heaven, and the clangour of music, like that of a mighty and triumphant host reverberated through all space, and the happy ones, more numerous than the sands of the desert, and more effulgent than eye hath beheld, gathered around the throne of Jehovah and his blessed Son, and a sound like that of a myriad chariots was heard, and the earth trembled; and the throne was lifted up and carried by Angel, and Cherubim, and Seraphim, towards heaven's portal. And the innumerable blessed gathered around the throne, and all the glory and terrible majesty departed on high, and the floor of heaven was closed.

And the great stars glared all fiery; and the bloody moon looked down; and the shorn sun hung ghastly pale amid terrible gloom.

And the evil ones that remained, more numerous than the sands of all the earth, smote their breasts, and tore their hair, and gnashed their teeth, in agony such as man never knew, saying, "Woe! woe! woe! and will it never again be day?"

And they cried for food, but found it not; and they howled for water, but there were no fountains, no rain, no dew! and they called for shelter, but there was no roof, no shadow! and they sought former friends, but friends spat upon them with curses. And those who asked for clothing, were covered with ice and snow, and shivered with intense cold; and those who wished for cool winds, were scorched by fiery blasts; lovers met each other with loathing and contempt; and parents and children approached each other in hatred. Servants scourged unjust masters, and were themselves scourged; and the idle lived in unceasing toil; and the gold of the miser was turned to blistering ashes, in which he was made to wallow without repose. And proud ones were eaten of vermin: and hypocrites were unmasked and cursed each other; and liars had their tongues cloven to the roots; the perfidious were continually betrayed into pit-falls, and they yelled in ceaseless dread; whilst slanderers were turned inside out; they were frightful and loathed even of the damned; and the place was one great hell! and an eternal tumult of weeping, and wailing, and cursing, and lamentation arose from the place. Some craved forgetfulness, but consciousness was ever present; some fain would try to hope, but despair was at hand; and all would have welcomed death, but they knew that death himself was dead, and swallowed up in victory, and again they howled in that dolorous hell.

And the dark world yawned, and a gulf was opened, and the damned went down, and were inclosed and shut up eternally, and were no more heard.

And there was a tempest, and a rushing of winds, and a pouring of floods, and rains, and hissing of lightning; and a howling of thunder; and flashing of meteors, and rushing of dread comets; and the blackened earth, shrivelled up like a burning scroll. And it was loosened from its orbit, and hurried through space, until it rested in a void, where neither sun, moon, nor star hath shone; there, unseen of God, and unknown of Angels, it should remain until creation was no more.

WALKS AMONGST THE WORKERS.

No. IV.

HEYWOOD AND HEAP.

THE slight sketch only which, owing to boisterous and excessively wet weather, I was enabled, in my last communication, to give of the important village of Heywood, left me ample room, as I considered, for further and more particular observations, and the result of those observations I now proceed to state.

Having a wish to visit Makeant Mill, (not Makin, as spelled page eighty,) I turned off to the right at Wrigley Brook, and traversed a good cindered road for probably about half a mile, away from the gloom and smoke, and right out into the open fields. On my left were retired winding paths along the bottoms and declivities of what, in spring time, are beautiful and verdant slopes, each with its rill of clear water hurrying to join the stream of the Roch, which floats, as yet, unseen, though we are within a few yards of its margin. In advance of us is a fold of houses, built somewhat in the form of a triangle; and just before we arrive at these we shall probably feel surprise at beholding on our left the black top of a square funnel or factory chimney, thrusting itself, as it were, out of the ground, and within a few yards of our track. That was the top of the chimney at Makeant mill. Of the mill itself we have, as yet, seen nothing, nor much of the land beyond, save some young woods on a sloping bank, and some tenter grounds, with white flannels drying in the wind. The place where the houses we have mentioned are situated is called "Back-o'-th'-Moss," and the houses themselves were the habitations of persons working at Makeant mill. A house of superior appearance marks the residence of the manager of the works. The houses of the workers seemed to have been built a considerable time; they were probably erected when the mill was enlarged, and first became a cotton factory. The interior appearance of some which I entered hardly bespoke so much of comfort, nor so good a system of housewifery, as many I had noticed in Heywood. But much allowance must, in such cases, be made for circumstances—for poverty, and mental and bodily depression. These poor people, I understood, had, during several previous years, been, sadly distressed for want of work, and had also much to complain of with respect to the absence of moral and social comforts. They were now differently circumstanced, and were beginning to reap the advantages of improved management. A little further than these houses is a row of good-looking modern cottages, including a provision shop and a public house.

Turning to the left, at the top of this triangular fold, we come, after advancing a few yards, within view of the valley and stream of the Roch, which here, after bending to receive the waters of the little brook Nadin (No-din, or silent water), pursues its course between the woods of Birkle and the steep and less wooded banks of Heap. After taking a glance at this fine, deep, and silent valley, with its lonely cottage at the bottom, and its broad straight stream gliding down, one is little prepared for any other objects save those of wild and unadorned nature; but one turn of the eye towards the left, and downwards, brings within our ken the roof of an irregular building, evidently a manufactory, from its chimney, and the form and arrangement of many windows. We descend then rapidly a good cindered cart-road; an old woman in a cottage directs us to the counting-house, where, if the gentleman, Mr. Clemishaw, who has had the management about eighteen months, be within, we shall receive any information which ought to be asked respecting the present state of the operatives, the nature of their employment, and the amount of their remuneration. I walked through every room of this mill, and I do say, that for cleanliness, good air, and the comfortable appearance of the workers, I never saw anything that exceeded it. It is a throstle spinning establishment, and employs about one hundred and eighty hands.

The boys of thirteen or fourteen years of age, were decently clad, and their clear, plump looks shewed they did not go to a scanty porridge dish at home. The girls and young women were as well looking. The youths and up-grown men were decent and cleanly; and the only drawback to my entire satisfaction in looking through the mill, was the observation that several of the married, child-bearing women, and women in years, seemed weakly and emaciated; some of the elder ones also were deformed, as if from weakness. But others of the married females looked quite well. The hands had been in constant work during the last eighteen months, and their earnings would average about nine shillings per week.

This mill was at first a small woollen manufactory; afterwards Sir Robert Peel, the elder, purchased it, and making some additions converted it into a cotton factory; it was the first which ever worked in the township of Heap. It has been frequently surmised that the present Sir Robert has a share in this and other manufacturing establishments in Lancashire; but such is not the fact, and Makeant mill, as well as a factory at Radcliffe, are the property of a relative of Sir Robert's.

As I ascended the road again, I could not but turn and enjoy another look of the valley; and I left the place with a wish that none of God's human creatures were worse off than those I had just seen in the old quiet-looking mill below.

From this place to the large manufacturing establishment of Messrs. Fenton, at Hooley Bridge, was but a step. On a sudden we come upon the edge of a deep bank of the Roch. Immediately below are the gas works; on the other side of the river arises the huge pile of building which the Messrs. Fenton have constructed for a manufactory. Numerous cottages extend in rows along the valley and beside the highway. One row in particular, below the mill, and above the stream, are fronted with spacious and neat gardens, and the whole together looks like a pretty new village, with a large workshop in the middle. I descended the bank and over the bridge, and observed that the houses were in decent and respectable condition, and judging from the appearance of the habitations, we might suppose that the inmates were all of the better class of work-people. I was prevented from entering the factory. A young man in the yard referred me for permission to Mr. Fenton, at Bamford Hall, or to Mr. Schofield, the manager, who was at home but indisposed. I preferred calling on the latter, and having explained the object of my visit to a servant, she returned with the message that my request "must have two or three days' consideration; I must call again in a few days." I told her I could not do that, and came away.

At four schools which I visited, viz: one built by Mr. Kershaw, a manufacturer, near Wrigley Brook; St. James's Infant and Juvenile Schools, and St. Luke's Infant School, I found remarkably fine and healthy children, to say nothing of their pretty and intelligent looks, of which their parents are no doubt a little proud already, and not without cause. I know something of Heywood, and have done so during forty years, but I must say, that I had never expected to have beheld in that place so fine a race of children as I saw this day; not a dim-looking shirt-collar did I observe, save on one boy, in the whole lot of about five hundred and fifty—not a smutty-looking face, except those of some two or three lads, who had probably soiled them at play. When the little folks held up their hands, which, at one school they did at the bidding of the master, and in the course of their daily exercise, it was really pleasing to behold so many innocent countenances beaming with joy, and their tiny fingers and palms as clean as were ever seen in human mould; and then their neatly-combed hair, and their clean apparel, were in keeping with the pure little beings themselves. Of one thing I felt satisfied, that however we might have changed as a community in some respects, the mothers of these children were an improved race decidedly; and would, doubtless, impart to their offspring a due portion of their advanced civilization and humanity. At the same buildings Sunday Schools are held, and about one thousand five hundred scholars attend on those days.

I next went into an extensive weaving shed, in which several hundreds of looms were at work. The hands differed but little in appearance from those I had seen at other places. I thought, however, that this shop was more crowded than any I had yet visited. A dust arose from the dried paste with which the warps had been dressed, and rested on every thing on which it fell: this would be some drawback on health. The further parts of the room appeared somewhat dim in consequence of the dust. This, however, might be accidental, and the result of the quality of some particular lot of flour, from which the paste had been made. In other rooms of the same mill I found the arrangements quite as good as any I had seen of the same description of manufacture. The carding-room was certainly "rather close," but not so much so as some I had entered. The scutching room was, as is usual, thick-aired, and dusty; about the same as are some places in a flour, or a logwood mill.

At Messrs. Cleggs and Hall's mill, there were about four hundred looms, weaving fustians of various descriptions. I went through one room, and observed the same appearances of general good health and personal neatness amongst the operatives as I had noticed at other places. Most of the weavers were young persons, and of those both sexes were employed—the greater part, perhaps, being females; others seemed to be married women and men, and some of the latter were overlookers. The place, I thought, was better aired than the last I had visited, but it was still crowded, and there seemed in this, as in other weaving shops, to have been the strictest economising of room.

An old veteran was pointed out who had been in many battles during the last war : he was also with Sir John Moore at Corunna. After the war he went to Canada, and had some land allotted to him on being discharged; but he left it, and returned to England, to end, as it seems, his days as a factory worker.

Standing at the door of this mill, and looking southward, we may catch an idea of the origin of the name of the township (Heap). A number of broad green mounds, exactly like tumuli, rise amongst the fields and meadows to a considerable distance. Some are larger, some are smaller than others, and Hind Hill, on which the residence of Mr. Clegg, one of the partners, is situated, appears to have been amongst the largest of the mounds on that side. The mill itself stands on what was originally one of these Heaps, but northward, towards Rochdale, several large ones have been cut into for sand, and now afford, as they long will do, a plentiful supply of that very useful article.

A WORD FOR MERCY.

O'er the moorlands wild and lone,
Comes a deep, and boding tone;
Reynard, coil'd within his den,
Hears the cry of dogs and men;
Whilst the poor beleagured hare,
Pants within her wilder'd lair;
And the bird with broken wing,
Dies in unknown suffering;
All to sport the lord who reigns
O'er the waters and the plains;
As if it indeed were joy,
Thus to torture and destroy.
Oh! would haughty man but know,
Mercy's mild and noble glow;
Surely, he would not distress
Beings God hath deign'd to bless.
Let the eagle tear his prey,
Leave the dog and fox, at bay;
And uplift thine eye of pride,
Where thine own oppressors bide.

A PETTY SESSIONS.

It is market day at the little town of Peelsborough, and you may observe country people coming in with their butter, and their eggs, and their garden herbs, and fowls to sell. The stalls in the new market, which has lately been erected by the noble lord of the manor, are all set forth in their most attractive forms: some with early fruit and vegetables; some with fish and game; some with clothing; some with crockery, and others with tin and hardware. The butchers have hung up their finest calves and sheep, whilst choice cuts of beef and pork are studiously arranged so as to catch the passers eye. The shops in the main street are all cleanly swept out; various articles are exposed in the windows and at the doors: weavers, hatters, and other operatives are taking home their work, and business at the taverns, and the various marts of sale has already begun.

But what means yonder crowd around a door at the lower end of the square? It is the petty sessions, a policeman informs us, and the magistrates have been some time on the bench; let us go in; were it only for a change of scene, and a short rest, it were perhaps worth the time expended.

The court-room is entered by a flight of high steps : it is in a building which is nearly new, and the arrangements for the court are very convenient. On our right is a crowd of people standing on the floor; before us, at the further end of the room is a table, with benches, on which are seated several attorneys, overseers, constables, and a police officer or two; a reporter for the newspapers is also there. The magistrates' clerk is in a compartment somewhat elevated above the table, and higher than him again, are the two magistrates, both of whom I know, personally, and believe them to be most worthy gentlemen in their private capacities. On our left as we stand, is the place for the witness, and on our right, the box, or compartment where the defendant is placed.

A young man, of the working class, but of very decent appearance, now occupies this unenvied position. He is charged with having unlawfully detained certain monies arising from the pledging of a watch. An attorney sits there for his defence; whilst another, right earnestly, for his client, is striving to get the lad convicted.

It seems that a widow, whom we will call Betty A., being in want of a trifle of money, borrowed it from the defendant, in security of which she left him a watch. The defendant kept the watch during a year or more, and he laid out some two or three shillings in repairing it. When he wanted his money, in consequence of being out of work, the complainant told him to pawn the watch in order to raise the money, and he sent another woman, Betty B., with the watch, who pawned it in his name, and gave him his money and kept the ticket; he not knowing but the owner had it. In the course of another year or so, the watch is wanted by the owner, who goes to the young man for it, and offers him the money he had lent, but refuses to advance the trifle he had expended in repairs. Meantime Betty B., who pawned it, had died, and on examination, it was ascertained that the watch had been pawned for some three shillings more than the sum originally lent on it. The young man at first refused to produce the watch until the whole sum was paid; he afterwards produced the ticket, and the watch was then found to have been pledged for three shillings extra, and so the case was brought before the bench. At one time there were strong indications of a determination to commit the defendant for felony, and the young fellow began to look rather anxiously about him; though not a tittle of evidence has been adduced to shew that he had ever seen or touched the three shillings extra for which the watch was pawned.

" I have known convictions in far slighter cases, at the New Bailey," said an overseer, to the defendant's attorney. " I have known transportation in cases no worse than this," said the clerk.

" I'll give them the three shillings, and have done

with them,"said the defendant's attorney; "I wouldn't," said another person; "I wouldn't give them three farthings; you'll ruin your client's character if you do, and there is not a tittle of evidence to connect him with the illegal money: wait, and let us see whether there will be a conviction on this testimony." He did so, and after much deliberation on the bench, the defendant was seriously admonished, and discharged.

The young fellow seemed astonished at the advice, he seemed not to understand it. "I know nothing about it, gentlemen," he said, "I never had"—"Come down," said his attorney, and the lad taking up his hat descended to the crowd.

An elderly man was next shewn into the defendants box, and his daughter, a rather pretty fresh coloured, country looking girl stood beside him; to speak for him, as she said. The defendant was a shopkeeper and farmer, residing in the neighbourhood, and the charge against him was having neglected to maintain his old father, who was incapable through age, and was supported by the parish. The young female advocate, with much self-possession, and an apparent absence of feeling for her more aged relative, pleaded that her father was not entirely his own person, but was, in a degree, deranged. The reply, by the overseer to that was, that if he were deranged, it was in consequence of being almost continually in a state of drunkenness. The girl then said the farm was not her father's, it was in her brother's possession. The overseer said if it did belong to the brother, it had been recently conveyed to him in order to lessen the present liability, and if that turned out to be the case, he also should be looked after.

The unnatural son—the defendant,—who was represented to be a person of considerable property, was, together with his pert and unfeeling daughter, reprimanded by the magistrates, but not half strongly enough; and the scene was concluded by an order being made on the son, for two shillings a week towards his father's maintenance.

Here was a spectacle for a christian country! a father produces hiᶜ daughter; a blooming, and apparently tender female, to plead against his father, and she stands up there, before a crowd, arrayed in her finery; with her ribbons and her frills, and her red rosy cheeks, and her eyes all unabashed, and tries with all her shallow art, to exonerate her father from the performance of a most sacred duty. Oh! what a shameful sight! and what a lesson to be remembered, should her father, in his old age, become dependent on her, or any other of his children! no wonder they said he was deranged! and though he shewed no signs of derangement, surely, he must be so, or he could not have consented to such an exhibition. Where could that poor mis-instructed, and heart-hardened girl have been schooled? she had certainly read her bible, and to how little purpose? how had all the good impressions given by her book, and her instructors been wormed from her bosom ? with what sort of a family could she have been associated ? what was the household, and the conversation, and the daily example before her, which could have so far obliterated all grace and tenderness from her heart. Talk of Hottentot missions, indeed ! when such heathenism is to be found at home.

The same overseer summoned the preacher to a new sect for non-payment of poors' rate. The defendant did not, like others similarly situated, take his place in the bar, but came at once and took his stand beside the attorneys table. He had a very sanctimonious air, which conveyed a notion that it had been practised before a looking glass. His dark locks were smoothed down, and parted from his forehead, and in his hand he held a small testament. When asked what he had to say against the charge of non-payment, he said the room he preached in was not liable to the poors' rate, inasmuch as it was a place of worship. The overseer said it was a school in the week-days, and the defendant preached in it on sundays, but it was not licensed, and therefore was chargeable with the rate. The defendant still contended for its non-liability ; and when asked by the magistrates, why, if such were the case, he did not appeal against the rate ; he said he could not appeal to any human tribunal, his religion forbad his doing so. On being told that he must pay the money, he opened his testament, and casting occasional glances towards the crowd of people—evidently with a desire to exhibit before them,—he proceeded to argue the point from scripture, but was interrupted by a question, which led to a rejoinder, and another attempt at a speech, which was again interrupted, and so on, for about an hour, when the magistrates, with some difficulty got rid of the litigant, by peremptorily ordering him to pay the rate. Never, probably, was there a finer specimen of specious obstinacy, and wilful, one-sided understanding. He went his way, not a little chagrined, his prepared sermon undelivered, and the money which he hoped to have retained, all but gone from his pocket.

A score or two of poor operatives were severally called for a like neglect, and took their places in the box. Some had been sick, and could not pay; some had heavy families to support; some had been visited by death in their families; and some had long been out of work. Their tales, though touching, and " owre true," were briefly told, and their cases as quickly despatched. There was no attempt at artful evasion, or pertinacious quibble; they mostly got off with an allowance of a fortnight wherein to pay the demand. That degree of patience and attention which had been undeservedly bestowed on the fanatic, was withheld from these poor people, and they were summarily dealt with.

A young fellow dressed like a mechanic, was next put up in the box, and the charge against him was the having stolen a number of files, the property of his employers, who were extensive manufacturers of engines and other machines. The files were produced and the superintendent of police stated that he found some of them under the cellar stairs, in the house of the prisoner's mother, and others at the house where the prisoner lodged. When the prisoner was arrested on the charge, he said, " the files had been left by his father, and if the police officer had lost as many things as he, the prisoner had, he would have put the files there himself." His father, it appeared, when living, was a block cutter, and occasionally a tool maker. A foreman from the shop where the prisoner had worked, said " the files were like those used at the place." One with a singular handle was shewn to him, and he was asked if he could identify that or any other of the tools ? but he said he could not, he could only say " they were like the files used at the shop." A piece of brown paper, in which the files were found wrapped up was shewn him, and he said that was the property of his employers; it bore their mark.

The prisoner still said the files had been left, with other tools, by his father at his death ; and the brown paper, he said, had been given to him by one of the book-keepers at the works, whose name he mentioned. He asked the book-keeper, he said, for a piece of paper to paste over a fire place, and the one given being too small, he wrapped the files in it. He offered to send for the man to prove this, if time were allowed.

He was committed for trial on a charge of felony.

A woman came timidly forwards and spoke to one of the police, who put her aside. She came again, and said she wished to know if bail could be taken for the prisoner. The official, speaking to the superintendent, said, they—meaning the prisoner's friends,—wanted to give bail; could they do it? " No, no," was the reply, and the woman was a second time put back. In a minute afterwards, rather doubtingly, and as a last resource, she made her way to the place where witnesses usually stood, and asked the magistrates clerk, " could they not put in bail ?" " Oh yes !" was the answer, and she quickly disappeared to find the sureties. The reporter for the newspapers, who had been out during most of the investigation, was now sitting at the table, and to him the superintendent of police handed a written paper, the substance of which appeared in a publication the day following, in these terms, the blanks being filled up in the newspaper.

" FELONY.—At the * * petty sessions, yesterday, (Friday) H. O. was charged with stealing a number of files and other articles, the property of Messrs. * * * & Co., machine makers. Superintendent * * stated that from information he had received, he apprehended the prisoner on the previous day. He then went to the prisoner's mother's, where he lived, in company with Inspector * * and in the cellar, under the stairs, they found the files, and other tools, wrapped in brown paper, which would be identified by * * foreman at the machine shop. After they had brought the files and tools to the office, he informed the prisoner where he had found them, and he admitting putting them there. A number of bricks had to be removed from under the cellar steps before the files could be got out. The property having been identified by the foreman of Messrs. * * * & Co., the prisoner was committed to the Salford Sessions for trial ! ! "

So here is a young man committed on a charge of felony, to support which, not a particle of evidence is produced. The files are found under the stairs, and he admits at once that he put them there, and says, if the officer had lost as many things as he had, he would have concealed the files there also. The foreman says, the files are like those used at their shop, but he cannot identify any of them; he cannot even say, that a singularly marked one, is the property of his employers. The prisoner is committed ! and then is handed in a report, that such a person was committed on a charge of felony, "the property being identified" as that of Messrs. * * * & Co., and so the lad is sent to prison, or bailed, and the report is read the day following by twenty thousand persons. And this is English justice, and Lancashire reporting, as performed on a certain day in March, eighteen hundred and forty-four; in the neat little country town of Peelsborough ! !

THE TRAVELLER.

CHAPTER IV.

AFTER the traveller had crossed the water, as already narrated, and had walked some distance, he became more collected, and then felt for the first time, that one knee was painful, and that he had a wound on his forehead ; but he did not consider them of much consequence, as, with the exception of a trifling halt, he was able to walk pretty well when the road was perceptible. Murky he found to be an excellent leader ; with his nose almost constantly on the ground, he soon discovered a path, and traced it without stopping, except when occasionally he waited for his master to come up, and with a faint whine invited him to follow. He therefore gave himself up to the guidance of his faithful companion, and followed him a considerable distance by the side of the stream, in the contrary direction from that they had before come. Afterwards Murky led him by a narrow path over several inclosures, next by the side of a wood, where the bray of an ass saluted his ears, and in a minute they were in a lane, and in company with a laden donkey, and a pedlar who was driving him.

" It's a dark night, sir," said the driver.

" It is, indeed;" replied the traveller.

" Get on, Billy," said the driver, giving his beast a tap with his open hand; " get on, and let us have company whilst we can."

" That you may easily," said the traveller, " for you see I don't walk very quickly."

" Ah, quick enough for the road, and the night," observed the driver, " it's not good to be in too great a hurry; 'more haste and worse speed,' as the old saying goes."

" But before I go much further, I should like to be quite certain as to what town or place we shall find at the end of our walk," said the traveller.

" Don't you know we are on the road to Brimbeck ? Are you a stranger in the country ? "

" Not properly speaking a stranger;" said the traveller; " I have been in this part before, but it is so long ago, that I am not certain as to where I am."

" Oh! you will find that out, if you will have a little patience," said the pedlar, " you will see the lights of Brimbeck ere long."

" I should think you are not a native of Lancashire," observed the traveller.

" No. I am from Staffordshire," said the man; " I was born, I believe, at Stoke, on Trent."

" And do you sell pots ? "

" I deal in many things, sir; a few pots, an umbrell or so, in wet weather: sometimes I tinker a bit, make swaps, or sell a little Sheffield ware."

" And you contrive to make a pretty snug living for yourself and your donkey ? " queried the traveller.

" Why we can hardly call it a snug living," said the pedlar, " though compared with the living that some humans and their brutes get, it is a snug one. We are up early and late you see to go our journeys; we are out in all weathers; we stand all chances; we call on all sorts of people, good, bad, and indifferent, and we find but few of the first; we wait at the doors of all sorts of dwellings, we encounter all kinds of company, drunk and sober, brutal and civilized, learned and ignorant, ragged and genteel, mean and honourable, hospitable and penurious. Aye! some would live and let live; give a man a chance of making a crust for himself, or a wisp for his poor beast; whilst others are voracious! they are ravenous-mad, sir, for gain; they can never have enough; they would suck in, myself, ass, panniers, old bones and all, so they could but, ' get something.' Oh; but theirs is a weary life; I would not change mine for it. No, nor do I think Billy would change with them either."

" You have a decent opinion of your donkey, then ? "

" Billy, sir, knows as well as myself, when he has to do with a human brute, with a brutal minded person

I mean; he knows, sir, a soft hand from a hard one; a pat on the back from a kick of the belly; a kind word from an unkind one; he knows all the doors where he gets a crust of bread; and though he don't pass compliments, I have no doubt but he is as thankful as those who palaver and make French bows; aye, aye, the poor dumb creature knows his friends, and I believe he respects them."

"I should suppose that you stand well in his favour," said the traveller.

"Why, I do now and then hit him, but only when he's lazy, and that's not often;" said his master. He fares almost as well as we ourselves do, sir; he eats of the same bread—for the children will give him their crusts,—he has as good a straw bed as I have, we give him boil'd tatoes, and take him in summer into the lanes, to the green grass, and in winter he lies indoors with us, and we make him warm mashes for his supper, and I don't know what more we could do for him. Aye, he knows his friends, sir; once I swapped him at Turton fair, to a coal-man, and the morning after, before day-break, what should we hear but a loud hee haw at our door. "That's our Billy, said I, jumping out of bed;" "it never can be Billy," said my wife; "but it is, said I, I'll pound it;" and sure enough, when I opened the door, there stood he, the poor brute, all miry, and as wet as if he had swum a pit: Come in, Billy, said I, and he gave one of his low grunts—as he will when he's pleased—just as much as to say, "Master, I am here again." Come in, Billy, said I, and he came in, and the children all got up—there was no keeping them in bed—and they made a fire, and gave him bits of bread, and he lay down amongst them on the hearth, and Billy and the children were as happy as kings."

"We'll never part with him again," said my wife. "I have parted with him, said I, he's sold, and I dare say the man will soon be here about him." "Well, let him have his own again," said she, "and give him a shilling or two for a rue-bargain; we'll not let Billy go again." And so it was like to be, for you see, she would have her own way; and when the coal-man came for him, which he did soon, he was about to lay a merciless stick on him, but I said, hold! hold, friend! till I've had a word or two with you; come, sit down, and he did so; and so, in the end, it was settled, and he led his old ass off, with two shillings extra in his pocket, and Billy has ever since been in our family."

"It's greatly to your credit that you behave kindly to the poor beast," said the traveller, "and more so that you cultivate the same feelings amongst your children; how many have you?"

"We have four," said the pedlar; "and though they are but rudely clad, and coarsely fed—that is coarsely, as they call it now a-days,—they get meat enough, and have all good health, and their common senses, thank God!"

"Those are great blessings," said the traveller. "though but seldom thought of as such."

"Aye! that's what I sometimes say to our neighbour weavers," observed the pedlar, "when they'r grumbling about every thing under heaven except themselves. I tell them not to look so much on the dark side of things: I tell them to cast their thoughts around, and try to reckon up all the good they enjoy, and make the most of it, instead of being eternally brooding over what they have not. Why Sam O' Ned's, the other day, was croaking as usual about the distress, and saying, " there were none that worked for their living, but were badly off." "Why now, Sam," said I, "to begin with thee, thou'rt not badly off; thou talks about what thou does not understand; thou'rt not badly off, I tell thee."

He said he was, and asked how I could prove to the contrary ?

"Well," I said, "thou hadst a breakfast before thou left home ?" he said he had; "and thou wilt have a dinner, I'll be bound ?" he said he should; "and thou wilt have a supper, when thou gets home ?" allowed; "and thou hast a roof to cover thee, and a bed to sleep in, may-hap ?" he said he had. "Well, and I'll be sworn, thou art as well dressed, as is many an Irish land-owner on a sunday; thou hast a decent cap on thy head, a coat without hole or patch on thy back, trowsers the same, stockings and shoes good enough to carry thee across England; and to my own knowledge, for I can see it, thou hast a good shirt—nearly new—next thy skin; what in the name of goodness is being well off, if thou art badly off?"

"Being well off," he said, "is being like those folks there, who are riding i'th omnibus; have not I as much right to ride as they have?" and then he began cursing great folks, as he called them.

"Thou hast," I said, "and thou may ride if thou'lst pay." Just then we were entering Toilington, and there sat a weaver at his jack loom, plying his shuttle like a machine, for it never ceased, and it flew almost as quick as thought; "look at that poor fellow," I said, and we stopped, and looked down through his cellar window, and there he sat, as white as a boil'd stewbone, as gaunt as a gre-hund, and as ragged as a scarecrow; working with hand and foot as yernstfully as if he were weaving by the mile, and death were on the road behind him, and the match were for life. "Look at him," I said, "there is one, who compared with thee, is badly off indeed! But what wouldst thou say if he were to come up here, and curse thee because thou hast a better coat on than he has; if he were to meet thee as thou returns, and abuse thee because thou hast earned more money than he can? What wouldst thou think of him, Sam?"

"I should think he was very unreasonable, to be sure," said Sam.

"Then never let me hear thee again reflect upon people, who are a little better clothed, and have a little more money in their pockets than thou hast. But let us go down and hear what this poor fellow says about his condition. And so Sam and me went down, and I said, "hallo, my good man, how do you do this morning?" and he said, "pretty well, thank you, I hope you are the same;" and I said, "why I'm pretty well at present, but this neighbour of mine complains sadly; he says he's very badly off." And with that the poor weaver gave him a look which I thought would have doubled him up.

"Badly off, indeed!" said the weaver; "that man badly off! well, to be sure, he looks as if he were. I thought I was badly off till this morning; cause if my shuttle runs from monday to saturday, I can't lay anything by at the week's end, and sometimes I am short, do whatever I will; yes, I thought I was badly off, but I don't think so now."

"And what made you alter your mind?" asked Sam.

"Come this way, and I'll shew you," was the reply; and with that he jumped off his loom, and went out at the back door, and we followed him. He led us into a lone back street, where sat a grey-haired, venerable woman, shaking with palsy, and almost blind. The place was very humbly furnished, but cleanly enough; and the old woman had a little fire in the grate, over which she was endeavouring to warm her shaking hands.

"How are you, Nanny?" asked our conductor.

"Why as weel as can be expected," said the old woman; "th' neighbours are very good! very good! one sent me her tea leaves, and another a bit of sugar, an' I've had a breakfast, thank God! an' th' o'erseer has been, and I expect something will be ordered for us this afternoon."

"I'm glad to hear it," said our conductor; "I think it's time something were done for you."

"It's happen all for the best," she said, "we cannot tell; we must wait the Lord's will, using our utmost endeavours in the meantime."

The rattle of a chain sounded up stairs, and soon after we heard a low moan. "Come this way," said our conductor, and we followed him into the chamber, where we found a young woman, her eldest daughter, chained and raving mad, on one side; and her youngest daughter, delirious with fever, in a bed on the other side of the chamber.

We came out of the house, and Sam looked at me. "This is not all," said the weaver; "that old woman, who has not a tear left to shed, lost two sons in battle; a third dishonoured himself by desertion; his sister went mad when she heard of it; and you see the rest. Now this is what I call being badly off," said the weaver; and with that he went into his cellar, shut the door, and the same instant, his shuttle was again in motion.

"I'll tell thee what, Sam!" I said; "it is not because thou art really distressed, that thou grumbles;

but because of the bad, envious, unthankful disposition thou hast got engendered in thy heart. Instead of enjoying, and making the most of what thou hast, thou turns sulky and makes an outcry about what thou hast not—perhaps never will have,—and certainly, in thy present frame of mind, canst not deserve to have. Like the dog with the meat in his mouth, thou drops thy realities to snap at shadows, and then howls at the consequences of thy own folly."

"But here we are at Brimbeck," said the pedlar, and with that he bade our traveller good night, and turning down a back street, he disappeared.

In a short time the young man approached a cottage that stood on the left, rather alone, and opening a garden wicket, he walked down and knocked at the door of the dwelling. He was bid to come in, and he did so, and found an elderly dame darning hose, and a young man, in the dress of a mechanic, sit enjoying his homely supper of oat-meal porridge and milk, whilst a cat, evidently a favourite one, lay basking on the warm hearth. The cottage was amply furnished with old fashioned chairs, tables, and other articles of the sort, whose well-polished surfaces reflected the gleams of the cheerful coal fire.

Both the inmates looked in apparent surprise at the intruder, and an exclamation of, "Bless us! what's to do?" escaped from the old woman, as she rose from her seat, and gazed more earnestly.

"Don't you know me?" asked the traveller,

advancing and holding out a hand to the aged dame. " I cannot say I do," she replied, keeping back, and peering at him with a candle which she had lighted. She saw him stagger a little, and thought he was tipsy: his appearance also tended to confirm that supposition, for his clothes were miry, and his face was streaked with blood; and surprised and alarmed, she continued to eye him, as he stood before her resting on his stick.

" You are surely Nelly Duerdin," he said, " I cannot be mistaken in that; and this is the cottage you lived in many years ago."

" I am Nelly Duerdin," she replied; " but I cannot call to mind who you are; still I think I must have known you; I have heard that voice before, somewhere."

" Ah! Nelly! Nelly! you are like all the rest of the world," he said, " you forget early friends; you don't know your nursling, master Richard."

" Master Richard!" she exclaimed, " master Richard! heaven bless you! you are him, indeed; you are my little brave, kind-hearted, naughty boy!" and putting down the light, she embraced him, and kissed his forehead, all gory as it was. " But what is the matter with you, my dear child?" she continued, " come, sit down; lay down on the couch-chair; what is the matter? you are all bloody and miry. Will, blow up the fire; we must have some hot water. And whose is that ugly dog? has he been worrying you? Bill, turn him out."

"No, no!" exclaimed the traveller; "don't, he is a friend."

"The dog is bloody too," said Will, who had been examining him by the light of the candle.

"I dare say he is," said his master; "poor fellow, he has done good service to-night; I will tell you all about it soon. But, Will! give me your hand," he said, "we are old play-mates, met once more!"

"I knew your voice the moment I heard it," said Will, "but for the life of me I could not make you out, in this plight; your brow is cut, and your lips are swelled."

"I dare say they are," said the traveller, "but don't trouble yourselves, it might have been worse."

By this time, old Nelly had drawn a jug of ripe ale, which the thirsty guest nearly took off at a draught, and thanked her for what he called "a blessed boon." His hurts were next examined, and bathed, and dressed, and some clothes belonging to his foster-brother Will, were taken out of the kist, and supplied the place of his soiled and bloody ones. A good cup of tea, and some boiled eggs were then set before him, and whilst he heartily partook the repast, he gave an account of his adventures since leaving the public-house at Webster-dyke; which narrative obtained for Murky, not only plenty of caresses, but a good supper; Will gave the dog the remainder of his porridge and milk, saying, "if it were the last meat he had in the world, he should share it with him."

" Did the men come to rob you, or to abuse you ? " asked old Nelly.

" I can't tell that," replied the guest, " I don't know what motive they could have to ill-treat me ; and as for robbing, I am not aware of having lost anything by their attack ; but I can soon ascertain that," and so saying, he went up stairs and examined the clothes he had doffed, and the linen he had on, when he found that a steel purse, containing a small sum in coin, a breast-pin, and a silver wrist-button, were missing. " Had they taken my pocket book," said he, opening it, and shewing a roll of notes, " I should have been somewhat more poor."

" Had they taken your life, which perhaps they would have done, had they known of those notes, it would have been far worse," observed old Nelly.

Various conjectures were hazarded by the dame and her son, as to who the robbers could be, and schemes were proposed for bringing them to justice, but the guest declared that he was not very anxious about that ; if they fell in his way, he might probably hand them over to a constable, but at present his mind was engaged on other matters, which he would talk over with his old mother when he had an opportunity. Will took the hint and soon afterwards went to bed, and a long and interesting conversation ensued betwixt the dame and her guest, which lasted until near midnight, when he rose, took the old woman affectionately by the hand, and said, " Thank God ! it is as I hoped ! as I

expected ! I can now rest indeed ; good night, my dear
old mother ! but mind ! not a word must escape—not
a word about my being here. I must sit in your back
room until I can get away. And dear Nelly, caution
Will, and don't let him go to work to-morrow ; I shall
want him to do me a trifling service." Nelly promised
to observe all he desired, and taking a candle, she
showed him to the little chamber in which he had often
slept when a boy; and there on a bed as hard as a
hermit's, but as white as a lily cup, he soon found that
repose of which he now began to feel the want, Murky
taking undisputed possession of the rug at his door.

WALKS AMONGST THE WORKERS.

No. V.

GREAT AND LITTLE HEATON.

ACCORDING to the returns of the last census, the townships of Great and Little Heaton contained one thousand three hundred and seventy-eight acres—one hundred and seventy-seven inhabited houses—ten un-inhabited—four in building—four hundred and ninety-one males—and four hundred and seventy-four female inhabitants. As it respects the extent of population, the Heatons are not, therefore, of much consequence, but, as exhibiting an interesting group of hand-loom weavers, these two small townships are worthy of notice. Here may be found the fancy and plain silk weaver, the weaver of cotton gingham, the weaver of strong, fancy, and plain nankeen, and, lowest in the scale, perhaps, the weaver of common umbrellas, which are next to calicoes in the lowness of wages, a large piece being woven for a few shillings. At present my notice will be confined to some of the poorest of these weavers, as exhibiting traits and positions worthy of the study of the artist, the philosopher, and the philanthropist.

The overseer, an intelligent and respectable man, represented the condition of the working population as being "very bad." He had been in the habit annually, of paying a particular visit of examination to the poor, and he had never found them in so bad a state as at present—many of them were actually starving, and how they contrived to carry on, day after day, he was at a loss to determine. Wednesday week was "a giving day," at the hall (Heaton Hall.) A quantity of clothing and bedding is annually distributed to the poor of the two townships, and of Pilsworth. The poor are visited and examined by the overseers, and those they recommend receive gifts of linen, woollen, blankets, and other articles, according to their respective necessities, but none are relieved except those belonging to the estate—the others must apply to the townships where they have a settlement. He never saw the poor people, he said, look so miserable before, when they came to be relieved. About seventy-two or three were relieved on Wednesday week, belonging to Great and Little Heaton, and about twenty from Pilsworth. I expressed a wish to see some of these poor families, and he very obligingly consented to accompany me, but first he would show me a family which had not received any relief from the hall, the reason being that the man had lived in his cottage a number of years, perhaps ten or twelve, without paying rent, and he was afraid, if he went to the hall, he should have notice to quit; and so he never went, and did not get any relief, as his neighbours did. The forenoon of Tuesday last was a kind of twilight in the country, the trees and hedges were thickly bearded by a hoar-frost.* We passed through several fields, and presently, in the looming of the grey, appeared an irregular mass, which at first seemed more like a hay-stack than anything else; this, however, was the habitation of the family we were going to see, and I will name it in my list,

No. I.—A very low old thatched house. The roof at one end had been blown off, or had fallen in, and the spars and timbers which remained sticking out, gave an idea of utter and naked desolation. Clusters of young elder trees grew around; a garden, or rather orchard, over-run with weeds, extended at the bottom of the dwelling; and a ditch, like a little moat, embraced the whole ruin on the side next the foot-path. What a habitation wherein to spend not a winter's day only, but a winter's season; aye, a long series of winters, when

> First comes the white hoar-frost at morn,
> Next comes the red sun, bald and shorn,
> Then comes the sleet, and then comes the snow,
> And then o'er the winter-fields howling doth go
> The cold, dark, wind, forlorn.

* This as before stated, was in the early part of 1841.

The roof formerly extended over two cottages, but one had, as before mentioned, become dilapidated ; and the other still covered, in some manner, a wretched family of seven persons, namely, the husband, the wife, his sister, and four children. We opened the low door, and entered a small dark room. " It's a cold morning," said some one in the place to my conductor, and I immediately shut the door, else my first wish had been to leave it open for the admission of light and air. On looking, as well as I could, through the dim, smoky mist of the place, the first object which caught my attention was a slender female of rather low stature, squatting before a fire of fresh gathered sticks, which she was trying to fan into a blaze. On her right sat another female, with a child on her knee ; on the hearth stood a boy ; and, sitting beside a wheel, near the door, was a fine little girl, with a cotton bonnet on her head. A low dim window admitted a faint light, which was more obscured by the escape of smoke from the sticks, and some articles of furniture which interfered. We could scarcely stand upright on any part of the floor, and in passing under the large beams we had to stoop. A few pieces of furniture, some much broken, and all of very primitive form, were scattered around the place. A stool or two, one or more old chairs, a wheel, a very few pots, a pan, and such like articles, seemed to be all the furniture and cooking utensils which the humble family possessed. As I stood looking on this group before the fire, my conductor put back a piece of what appeared to be old sacking, which hung against the wall; he went behind it, and beckoning me to follow, disappeared. We entered a place in which the beams seemed about to fall and crush us; two small low windows admitted very scanty light to two looms, in each of which was a warp of cotton gingham. A few moments passed before I could detect any being in the place except myself and friend. At length something like a human head moved, and I found that a weaver was there, "getting up his rods." When he stood up, and I could see him better, I perceived that he was a tall man, about thirty-five years of age, thin and pale looking, and with rather a heavy cast of countenance. I questioned him about his work, and he said it came to fourteen shillings a cut, and he could weave one in three weeks. I mentioned the apparent insecurity of the building, and he said it certainly did rock a little, when the wind blew, but he minded not that; it was secure enough, and he should be well satisfied if he could only get a little straw wherewith to thatch it! I asked him about the chamber, and my conductor led me up five or six wooden steps, and into a small dark loft, more like a hen-roost than a sleeping-room for a human family—in fact, it was a hen-roost as well, and a fine poot jumped off one of the bed's feet as we entered. "He has four hens and a cock," said my friend, when I expressed my surprise at finding a hen perched there. A small window admitted a gleam of light into the place, by which I could see that on either hand, and almost close to the thatch, stood an old bedstead, covered with a dark-coloured mass of what appeared to be coarse, dirty sacking, but which was certainly all the bedding this wretched family possessed. I could not but advert, in thought, to some of the comfortable houses which I had seen at Heywood—to those which I knew were enjoyed by the weavers of Middleton and the spinners of Crompton; and I mentally remarked, "If this man had such a home, how happy, how grateful he would be!" Yet he wished only for "a little straw to thatch his cottage!" "He won't apply to the guardians," said my conductor, as we returned; "he is afraid they would put him in the union workhouse, and he assuredly would perish with his family in yonder place before he would be separated from them." He further said, he did not believe the family had more than sixpence a week each to live upon. They generally came to his shop in the morning for two pound and a half of meal, which cost fourpence halfpenny, and that was chiefly what they subsisted on till the following day, and so they continued. He also said, it was probable the cottage would be pulled down next spring; it was unfit to live in, and the materials would be made use of for draining and fencing. No. 2, or the second family we visited, had only two looms, and one was without work. The family were five in number, and they seemed to be in poor circumstances. No. 3, had two looms empty, and two with work in; the family were seven in number, and were all up-grown; they, however, appeared to be poorly situated. No. 4, had two looms empty, and two at work, with seven children. No. 5, had four looms, all at work; a family of thirteen persons; and seemed better circumstanced than some of his neighbours. No. 6, had a family of six persons, viz: wife and self, and four young children. Had two looms, (cotton), both at work, one with gingham, and one with umbrella, and the latter was paid at the rate of about eight shillings for eighty yards. He was betwixt thirteen and fourteen years in the army, and received three wounds, viz: two at the storming of Badajos and one at Albuera. Was also at the battles of Salamanca, Vittoria, Roncesvalles, the Pyrenees, Orthes, Toulouse, and at New Orleans. "Was very lucky in seldom being sick, except from wounds;" was nearly always on duty, and in most of the battles fought in the Peninsula and America. Was discharged without pension, in consequence of going for limited service. "The old lord," at Heaton, (the first Earl of Wilton), would have got him a pension had he not fell ill and died, and a kind of clerk, at Bury, cheated the poor fellow and others out of their tickets and prize money. Surely the guardians of the union at Manchester might do something for this deserving man, were it only, as I observed, "to keep him off the township." "He is not on the township," said my friend the overseer, "he has had a large family to provide for, and he has had but a very few shillings off the parish."

Some women were lading water at a fine clear well by the road side, and my conductor informed me it was the " Katty Green Well," and the hollow where we stood, was " The Katty Green." I asked the woman if the water made good punch ; they said they had not tried it, and one said she had never seen whisky. We entered a very old, but well-thatched cottage ; like the first I visited, it had a large garden attached, and was fenced off with a hedge of young elder trees. The inside was about the same, with respect to space and elevation, as the one before noticed, but this was much more cleanly, and was also better lighted and furnished. This, indeed, was a comfortable warm place in comparison. A young woman, who stood on the hearth, said it was called " Katty Green Hall." I remarked, that at a hall there was often a lord and a lady, and she, laughing, said she was the lady. I asked where was the lord, then ? and she, still laughing, said, " that was him," meaning a light, low-set man, who was in the act of pulling a drying iron out of the good coal fire. I observed that there must be a chamber, but I could not see any road to it. I was, however, soon shewn a ladder of three or four stones, reared on the other side of the hob, which the lady had to ascend when she went to her dressing-room. This place, my conductor informed me, was now a freehold. It originally, or so far back as could be traced, belonged to a family named Holt, which merged in a single young man named William, who was seen going towards Rochdale one Sunday morning, and never returned or was again heard of. The parish officers, after a time, broke into the premises, but found no clue as to his retreat or the disposal of the property. It is to be supposed there were not any acknowledged relatives, or at least any who chose to claim property which was perhaps considered disputable. There were two cottages at the time, and the parish put in them two pauper families, who occupied without paying rent or any acknowledgment. One of the cottages was blown down some years since, and the remaining one had been in the occupation of the present possessor, his father, and grandfather, during eighty years, and, of course, was as good a freehold as any in England.

SONGS OF THE LANCASHIRE DIALECT.

The celebrated song of Joan O' Grinfilt, beginning

"Sed Joan to his wife on a wot summer's day."

Of which, perhaps, more copies were sold amongst the rural population of Lancashire, than of any other song known, has been generally ascribed to the pen of James Butterworth, the author of a poem, called "Rochervale," and other productions of considerable literary merit. The writer of this, long held the common opinion as to the origin of "Joan." The song took amazingly; it was war-time; volunteering was all the go then, and he remembers standing at the bottom of Miller-street, in Manchester, with a cockade in his hat, and viewing with surprise, the almost rage with which the very indifferent verses were purchased, by a crowd which stood around a little old-fashioned fellow, with a withered leg, who, leaning on a crutch, with a countenance full of quaint humour, and a speech of the perfect dialect of the county, sung the song, and collected the halfpence as quickly as he could distribute it. Some years ago, the writer fell in with this same personage at Ashton-Under-lyne, and took the opportunity for acquiring further information respecting the origin of a song once so much in vogue. He accordingly invited the minstrel to a little rest and chat at a neighbouring tavern, where over a pipe, and a pot or two of ale, he learned all he wished to know on the subject, which he noted down in short hand as the narrator gave it.

It was a cold and rainy day in winter; the door was accordingly shut, the fire stirred up to a warm glow; the cripple sat basking before the fire with his lame leg thrown across his crutch, his other foot on the fender, when after putting a quid of the tobacco into his mouth, and taking a swig of the ale, he went on gaily with his narrative for some minutes, until glancing towards the paper and seeing uncouth figures multiplying upon it, he sprung on his one foot, and with a look of astonishment, not unmixed with concern, he exclaimed, " Heigh ! heigh ! theer ! I say ! wot mack o lett-ters arto settin deawn ? theer I say ? wot dusto ko thoose lett-ters ? dusto think at nobody knows wot theawrt dooin ? busithe, I'd hathe to know, at I know wot theawrt doin az weel az theaw dus thisel. Theaw pretends to rule th' plannits, dusto ? busithe I con rule um az weel az theaw con, an that I'll let-te know, iv theaw awses to put ony othe tricks o' me."

A hearty laugh, a brief explanation, and more than both, a kindly invitation to the drink and tobacco, soon brought the guest to his seat again, and to his wonted jovial humour. He then said there were thirteen "Joan's O' Grinfilt" produced within a short time; but the original one,—that above mentioned—was composed by Joseph Lees, a weaver residing at Glodwick, near Oldham, and himself,—Joseph Coupe— who at the time of the composition was a barber, tooth-drawer, blood-letter, warper, spinner, carder, twiner, slbber, and rhymester, residing at Oldham. He said they were both in a terrible predicament, without drink or money to procure any, after being drinking all night. They had been at Manchester to see the play, and were returning to Oldham the day following, when, in order to raise the wind, they agreed to compose a song to be sung at certain public-houses on the road, where they supposed it would be likely to take, and procure them what they wanted, the means for prolonging their dissipation. A storm came on, and they sheltered under a hedge, and the first verse of the song was composed by him in that situation. Lees composed the next verse, and they continued composing verse and verse, until the song was finished as afterwards printed; but it took them three days to complete it. They then " put it ith press," and he said, " we met habin worth mony a hunthert peawnd iv widdin had sense to ta'care oth brass.

RADCLIFFE OLD HALL.

THIS interesting relic of old English domestic architecture was taken down a number of years ago to make room for a row of cottages for the workpeople of Mrs. Bealey and Sons, bleachers. It is understood that the Earl of Wilton, to whom the place belonged, sold the materials to the above parties, and rented the land to them, and so, in the spirit of modern improvement, the order was given, "take it down, why cumbereth it the ground." This venerable pile was highly interesting to all who loved to gaze on the relics of other days; and it was probably calculated to convey a more correct idea of the rude but strongly built habitations and festive halls of our forefathers than any other object to which the curious of this neighbourhood had access; and by them, no doubt, its destruction has been much regretted. Sir Walter Scott directed public attention to Haddon hall, as a representative of the halls of the early Norman or latter Saxon chiefs, but the hall at Radcliffe must have been much older than Haddon hall, as Sir Walter describes it. The materials at Radcliffe, were chiefly beams and planks of solid black oak, which, together with the simplicity of the construction, and the rudeness of the workmanship testified to the great age of the edifice. What a pity that it could not have been let alone, or rather that it was not deemed worth a little expense and trouble in covering it in once more ; that it was not given as a shelter to some half dozen poor families, on condition of their keeping it in perfect order : it would have thus endured for ages. The square tower, or fortified part of the ancient residence, still remains, but tottering with decay. The vaulted roof of the lower room almost hangs by a single stone, and unless it be protected from further wanton outrage, it must soon share the fate of the hall, and leave only its name in the remembrance of things that have been.

THE TRAVELLER.

CHAPTER V.

THE following morning betimes, Jonathan Handy, the overlooker of Mr. Staidley's mill, at Brimbeck, was waiting for him, when he came down stairs at his house at Glyeminside.

" An incident has just now come to my knowledge," said Jonathan, when Mr. Staidley asked his business, " which, though it be trifling as compared with some of our events, I thought it best to communicate it to you without delay.

Before the mill started I accidentally heard two of the hands talking, and one said to the other, ' I could like to beg off for to-day, I must ask Jonathan about it at breakfast time.'

' Pho!' said the other, ' If I'd a mind of a holiday, I'd have one, and never bother Jonathan about it.'

' I'll not go without leave,' said the first; ' we'er very busy with these new frames.'

'And suppose Jonathan won't give you leave,' said the second.

'Well then I must stop at work,' said the other. 'I'll not go away without permission; I'm sure if I can show any fair and good reason why I should go, neither the master nor Jonathan will deny me; and I think if I'm hard pushed I can show a reason that won't easily be denied.'"

"And who were those hands?" asked Mr. Staidley.

"The one who wanted to be off, was Will Duerdin," said Jonathan, "and the other was Yedd Burfielt, whom we shopped last week."

"You have done rightly in coming up to inform me. The circumstance, though apparently but of small consequence, affords traits of character which we should never lose sight of," said Mr. Staidley. "Such things are not trifling, though they are commonly deemed so; they are the indicators of feelings, which combined, affect both ourselves and our operatives either for good or for evil. Let us never lose an opportunity, Mr. Handy, of cultivating amongst our work-people a right trustful confidence, in the good and considerate intentions of your management and my supervision. It is well to have the machinery going and in good order; it is well that we make a profit by our productions; but it is far better, if conjointly with these things, we can so deal with our workpeople as to make them our friends. Just we will be, whilst I have the mill, and kind in all reason,

when possible. You know my views Mr. Handy, and
1 believe I can depend on your best endeavours to
give them effect. The reply of Will Duerdin affords
another instance of the good resulting from the system
we have hitherto acted upon. Let us continue it, and
if possible still further increase that confidence and
attachment which our people have on more than one
occasion manifested towards us."

"I shall always be most happy, sir, to be the instrument for carrying your honourable intentions into effect," said Jonathan, "and in pursuance of that
pleasing duty, I determined to make known to you
Will's conduct this morning."

"He has not yet spoken to you?" queried Mr.
Staidley.

"No; but I expect he will when the engine stops
for breakfast."

"I am glad you have told me," said Mr. Staidley.
"Will shall have his holiday, but when he speaks to
you, you can say he had better ask me about it."

"I will do so," said Mr. Handy, as he left the room,
but recollecting himself he asked "should any notice be
taken of Burfielt?"

"Yes," said Mr. Staidley, "by all means; should
he ask you for any reasonable favour, be sure to let
him have it. Let him understand practically, that he
need not go off without asking; that he need not be
afraid to 'bother Jonathan about it,' for that if he 'can
show any fair and good reason,' as Will Duerdin said

for any favour he wants, he will not be denied. After
two or three proofs of our wish to oblige him, and
when he has had ample opportunity for understanding
our system, should he then absent himself without
leave, the consequences must be on his own head, and
he must be made to feel them. At present, however,
don't appear to notice him more than another; we
should not think hard of him as yet; he may have
learned from bad examples where he came from."
And with these instructions Jonathan departed.

Mr. Staidley and the ladies were at breakfast, when
a servant made known that William Duerdin wanted
to see master if he was at liberty.

"Show him here," said Mr. Staidley.

Will made his appearance, and was saluted with a
good morning by his employer; "Good morning, sir,"
said Will; the ladies nodded and smiled; Miss
Staidley motioned him to take a seat, and asked kindly
about his mother, and Will respectfully answered her
enquiries.

"I wanted to beg a favour this morning," said Will
to Mr. Staidley, after the introductory remarks were
over.

"What favour wouldst thou have, Will?" asked
Mr. Staidley.

"I wish to beg off work to-day," said Will, "if you
would be so kind."

"And could not Jonathan have done that for thee?"
asked his master.

" I went to Jonathan," said Will, " and he said I had best see you about it, and so I made bold to come up."

" Very good," said Mr. Staidley, " I know Jonathan is a considerate man. And pray Will, what is it that makes thee wish to leave work at this busy time."

" A very particular friend, both of mine and my mothers came to Brimbeck last night, and he wishes to have my company to-day, if you please, sir."

" Aye, let Will have his holiday, brother, if you possibly can," said Miss Staidley.

The master remained silent, and seemed to be considering.

" I'll fetch the time up ith next fortnight," said Will.

" Don't make thyself uneasy about that," said Mr. Staidley, " I am disposed to grant to any of my hands whatever indulgence they can in reason ask for. Thou knows, Will, we are busy about the new frames, and, under the circumstances, I think I should be assured that a holiday is necessary to some good thou hast in view, or at least that it will not be spent in a manner entirely unprofitable to thee. I think the benefit, whether from pleasure or business, ought to be somewhat nearly commensurate with the worth of thy time, and my loss of thy immediate labour. I wish not to pry into thy private affairs, but tell me, Will, how is it likely thy day will be spent ? will it be spent in mere pleasure, or business, or in both ?"

"In both, I hope," said Will, "for my business will be a pleasure. The gentleman—the friend I mean,—has not been at Brimbeck these last five years, and I'm sure the rendering of a service to my hon——, honest comrade," said Will, embarrassed, "will afford me great satisfaction."

Miss Staidley put down the coffee pot rather suddenly; her hand shook that she could not hold it, and the colour went and came on her cheeks. Mr. Staidley did not notice the circumstance, though others did, for, turning in his chair, he said, "Will, take thy holiday, and I wish thee all pleasure with it; but if thou be merry with thy friend, don't forget to be wise."

"I thank you, sir, and if necessary, I will remember your good advice," said Will; as he made his bow and left the room.

"Well, I'm sure! master Will Duerdin," said Lissy, the servant maid, as Will took up his hat and was leaving the kitchen. "Well, I'm sure, but some folks are very high this mornin, an going away without so much as good bye, or the sperrin of one civil question."

"I really am in a hurry, Lissy, else, you know there is not a lass within miles o' Glyeminside, with whom I would rather have a five minutes chat, or a ten minutes whisper at any time than with Lissy Estain."

"I know nothin oth sort, nor do I believe it, only you think you'll make up for your skulkin away, by a a bit of flam, as usual; if you were so desirous of a chat, or a whisper, as you say, why, it's not so very far, fro Brimbeck to Glyeminside."

"Well, but Lissy, excuse me this mornin. I shall be up again before long, I dare say; at present, a friend, a stranger in a way, is waiting for me."

"A friend? what sort of a friend? is it a he friend or a she friend that you are in such a hurry about? I should think it is the latter."

"Well, it's a he friend," said Will, impatient to be gone; "it's a gentleman"—our young master,—he said, but correcting himself—"it's one I've not seen these last five years. So good bye, Lissy; mayhap I may see a bonny ribbon that will please somebody, ere long;" and with that he hurried away.

Will did not retreat so suddenly, but Miss Staidley, who at the moment came out of the parlour, caught a glance of him as he left the door; the servant also, she thought, was in a rather musing mood, and the latter, on seeing her mistress, betrayed some confusion.

"What were you studying about, Lissy?" said Miss Staidley, in her usual good tempered, free way.

"Why, mam; I was thinking about what Will Duerdin said before he went," replied Lissy.

"And what might that be?" asked Miss Staidley.

He said that a young gentleman,—a young master —I think it was master—was waiting for him, and he was in a great hurry.

"A young master, was it?"

"I think it was master; at any rate he said mast—

and then he stopped, as if he could not get the word out of his mouth."

"Did he not mention a name?" asked Miss Staidley.

"No, he only said," 'a young gentleman; young master;' and then he stopped himself. "Oh yes, he said, ' our young master.'"

"Lissy, open the door; what a hot fire you have," said Miss Staidley, as she took a seat on the couch-chair.

"Sure, mam; you said we must roast the beef for dinner, and we'er quite out for bread, so I thought I'd best heat the oven."

"Yes! yes! I know you must; you'll do what's proper, Lissy, I have no doubt; only just water that plant there in the window; and Lissy, let me have a drop also."

As Will was hastening home, he overtook Yed Burfielt, who was returning to work after breakfast. "Well," said Yed, "didto ax Jonathan obeawt gettin off for to-day?"

"1 did," answered Will.

"On did he githe lyev?"

"He did not," said Will.

"I towd the heaw it wud be," said Burfielt, in a kind of triumph, "I knew theaw'd never get lyev, iv theaw axt for it."

"But I have gett'n lyev," said Will.

"Heaws that? theaw sed he wudno give it the."

" But th' mester gan it mhe," said Will.

" Why, an hasto bin at th' mester, then?" asked Burfielt.

Will said he had, and that he was so well satisfied with the course he had taken, and with what Mr. Staidley had said to him, that he would never attempt himself, nor advise any other of the hands to leave work without asking leave.

" That's thy way," said Burfielt, as he smiled rather contemptuously at Will, and turned down towards the factory.

When Will got home, he found his mother and master Richard at breakfast in the little back-room ; and he streight made known to them the result of his application, and they both launched forth in praises of his good employer.

" I'll tell thee what I've been thinking about," said master Richard.

Will intimated attention.

" I find I'm not much the worse for last night's rough and tumble; my knee is stiff, and my face is bruised and disfigured, which latter circumstance is favourable to my project. Thou shall get a gig or a car, and a horse, as good as thou canst have for money, and instead of dispatching thee on my business, I'll go with thee."

" Very good," said Will ; " I'll have a tit and a vehicle of some sort at the door in a short time."

" Make a good breakfast first," said master Richard, " and then be as quick as you please."

In a few minutes Will had left the house to seek a conveyance, and master Richard eyeing himself in the glass, said, " he was sure no one would know him."

" There will not be any danger of that," said Nelly Duerdin ; " you are next to my own child, and if I met you on the road a hundred times, I should not know you."

" That will do," said master Richard; " I shall be relieved from confinement here, and shall the better be able to fulfil my friend's commission, without the whole country being aware of my sojourn in these parts."

Will Duerdin was not long in dispatching his errand ; he found a neat vehicle, and an excellent horse, which Mr. Thumbroad, the hosier and draper, let him have for the reasonable consideration of a guinea. Will knew there was no time for haggling, and so he assented to the modest demand, and in less than an hour after he came from Glyeminside, he and master Richard were on the high road to Webster-dyke.

It happened the same forenoon, that Miss Staidley discovered they were without a vast number of articles which were wanted in the house ; she therefore, very properly, would go down to Brimbeck and order them, and she did go down. Nelly Duerdin's garden gate stood open as she got to the bottom of the lane, and though she would have been glad to chat with the old woman—as she generally did—she felt a kind of inward consciousness restrain her from visiting the cottage that morning ; accordingly she passed forward into the village, and after doing business at several places, she called at Tryscales, the grocers, and was immediately attended to by the mistress of the house.

" I wonder who Nelly Duerdin has had to breakfast this morning," said Mr. Tryscale, to a respectable looking customer at the other counter.

" I don't know I'm sure," said the man; " I have not heard of any visitor."

" She came here for lump sugar and mocha coffee," said Tryscale, which she never buys for her own use; and she got change for a bank-note."

" Some one must have called to see her then," said the other ; perhaps some of her London acquaintance."

" I should rather think not, from so high a quarter as that," said Tryscale, " for in a short time after old Nelly had been here, her son Will went down the street with another man in a gig."

" Did he so ?" said the customer, " that would probably be Mr. Plugman, the engine maker ; young Duerdin, I believe, sometimes goes with him on business for the mill."

" No, it was not Plugman, I know him," said Tryscale; " this was a different kind of person ; a snub-nosed, thick-lipped man ; with a top-coat on, and a shawl tied nearly over his ears."

" That couldn't be Plugman," said the other.

" Oh no, it wasn't Plugman ; but we shall be hearing in the course of the day. They seemed in a hurry," said the grocer.

At this stage of the conversation, Miss Staidley, having given her orders, left the shop, and proceeded towards home in a somewhat more calm state of mind than she left it. It was evident to her, that whoever it was, with whom Will Duerdin was associated for the day, that person was not the one whom Will's confused manner, and half intimations, had led her to expect; and, that particular individual being thus set aside, there was no other that could interest her feelings. Thus she was returning home in a state of tranquility, which but a short time before, she did not expect to have enjoyed on that day. When going up the main-street, her ears were assailed by a confused noise, and she presently met a crowd of persons, chiefly composed of boys and girls, with a hundred or two of young and up-grown men. They advanced at a hurried pace, and it was said they came from Toilington, and were going round to stop all the mills. Whenever they passed a provision shop, or met a person of respectable appearance, they set up a shout, and when Miss Staidley stepped aside on the foot-path the shout was repeated; one or two called to her by name, whilst others used words of threatening import, with something added about the mill, and so the crowd rolled on. But some stragglers of a worse class hung on the outskirts and rear of the mob. These were men of a suspicious appearance, and females of a hardened and abandoned demeanour; they went into shops and houses, stealing, craving charity, or intimidating;

they even stopped persons in the street, and by cajolery, reproaches, or threats, endeavoured to levy contributions, and in many instances they succeeded. A ruffian of this class accosted Miss Staidley, and taking hold of her reticule, asked her in an almost menacing tone, " to leave a trifle for the poor women, who were almost dropping it'h' street for want of something to eat."

Miss Staidley twisted the strings of the reticule round her hand, and grasping it more tightly, with rare firmness, asked the man, " whether he intended to beg or to rob ?"

" Oh ! to beg, certainly, mam," said the fellow, quailing before her calm, determined look.

" Then let go my property," said the lady, " and ask in a civil manner," and with that the man loosed his hold of the bag.

" Oh ! that's one o'th Staidley's," shouted a virago ; " the rich Miss Staidley, an all they have in the world they've got out o poor foke."

" Leave her to us," cried another woman, " off with her furs," said a third ; " strip her," shouted another; " up with her fine veil, and let her look th' cowd day ith face, same as we do," vociferated another amazon, from the further side of the street. And thereupon, several of the women came around Miss Staidley, and were in the act of removing her bonnet and fur tippet, when a young woman suddenly grasped the locks of one, and tore her to the ground, and a blow from a crutch paralyzed the arm of another, of the assailants. " The

hands! the hands!" was shouted down the street;
"Staidley! Staidley!" was echoed from the other end,
and in that instant a fierce battle was gathered around
the astonished, though not affrighted lady; and in one
minute the thievish hangers on of the mob were
beaten, routed, or in custody.

When the mob appeared before Mr. Staidley's mill,
to which they proceeded direct on entering the village,
the hands were about going to dinner. Most of the
men and boys stopped to hear what the mob was about,
and a kind of meeting took place near the mill: the
women and girls, however, went their way, and a body
of them having to pass along the street they came up
just at the time the mob followers were abusing the
sister of their employer, "Now lasses! will you stand
by and see that?" asked an old woman, pointing with
her crutch; and ere another word could escape, the
onset before described was made on the despoilers, and
a few men joining the factory women, the whole body
of thieves and prostitutes were disposed of as before
narrated. The young women, and the men then formed
around Miss Staidley, and insisted on escorting her
towards home, until she was out of danger. "Oh! I
wish I could go with you," said an old woman, who
came hobbling out of the kennel on her crutch. She
was Nelly Duerdin, the leader of the onset, and they
all gave a shout, and gathered about her, and praised
her, telling Miss Staidley how the brave old woman
had acted. Miss Staidley spoke very kindly to her,

and asked if she had received any injuries, and being assured she had not met with any mischance save a roll in the gutter, she would have had the old woman home with her, but she begged to be let off; and so, Miss Staidley, charging some of her friends to see her safely home, she, with her escort, left the village and ascended the hill towards Glyeminside.

At parting, she stopped and thanked them most emphatically, telling the women she would give them an early proof of her gratitude, and the men, that a full representation of their conduct should be made to her brother, who, she doubted not, would find some means of marking his sense of their desert.

THE TRAVELLER.

CHAPTER VI.

NOT deeming it necessary to describe Mr. Staidley's mill minutely, we will merely say that it was considered a large establishment, for that part of the country. Besides the usual appearances of a manufactory, it was well white-washed, both inside and out, and the wood-work of the building was painted and in good repair; the windows also, were constantly cleaned, and the hands generally, falling in with their employers wishes, took a pride in the respectable appearance of their huge workshop. It had cost the proprietor, as may be supposed, some time, and many exertions to create, and improve so desirable a feeling amongst his operatives: every practicable thing, which, so far as was known, could add to their health and comfort during working hours, was supplied; and whenever a workman or other person offered a useful suggestion, it was acknowledged with thanks, and attended to. The apartments were lofty and roomy; the machinery chiefly new, and that, together with the floors, and all within the building, was kept fastidiously clean. The moving geering was boxed off, where practicable or necessary; besides which, strict rules were laid down, and rigidly enforced, for preventing any save authorized persons from meddling with it. In addition to these, no man or boy, was allowed to work in the place, with his shirt sleeves exposed, or an apron on, or the ends of a handkerchief dangling from his neck; all the females wore long pinafores, or vests, with close sleeves at the elbow, and tied in several places behind, so that their garments could not become entangled in the machinery; they were also forbidden working with their hair loose, and if they wore it in combs, or in ringlets, as most of the younger portion would, they never entered their working room without previously putting on a cap, generally of fine network, which fitted close to the head, and fastened with a clasp on one side; every female must work in a cap of some sort. All those who were employed on the ground floor of the mill were expected to wear wooden clogs whilst at work, unless tender feet made them inconvenient. This was done with a view to guard them against the possibility of ill effects from cold or damp, though, the lowest rooms at Brimbeck, did not in those respects, present any extraordinary exception to the general condition of such places. " Our Christopher," the workpeople would sometimes say, " cares as much for us as if we were his children."

The mill was situated on the bank of a deep and generally placid, though not very broad stream, which was sometimes visited by floods, when heavy rains, or sudden thaws had taken place in the uplands. A low wall surrounded the mill on the land side, and fronting a lane which led from Brimbeck, stood a lodge, and a pair of gates, marking the main entrance to the works. A school and several rows of neat cottages, all white, and with gardens attached, stood at a short distance from the factory; other cottages in various situations, and at greater distances, were interspersed amongst fields, and on the hill sides; these were the residences of some of the workpeople, whilst others occupied tenements in the streets and old garden lanes of the village.

The refuse of the mob having been disposed of as before described, the main body, after parading the village, collected near the closed gates of the mill, and as the hands returned from dinner they became mingled with the crowd, and various arguments and wordy contentions were going on when a person on foot was seen descending the hill at some distance.

" It's Staidley ! " was murmured amongst the crowd.

" Let him come ; who cares for him, or the likes of him," said one of the leaders, an Irishman, who stood on a fence by the road side.

" He will come," said a stout man in a soiled

jacket, in reply to the spokesman; "he will come, and he shall return when he chooses; Chris Staidley is not going to ask either Shuffleby's or their hands, or any mob fro Toilington, whether he must come to, or goo fro his mill."

"We'll try that," said the leader, "peaceably if we can, forcibly if we must;" and stooping to some men below him, he said, "mark that fellow who stands prating at the gates;" and several moved forward, and stood near the man.

"Oh! I know him," said one, "he was a skulker during th' last turn-out." "It's Dick O' Brella," said another, "as great a nobstick as ever lived."

"You're a brace o' liars," said Dick, "an yo' need not ha come to Brimbeck a bein towd so."

"A nobstick! a nobstick!" shouted several voices.

"Where," said some; "pummel him," said others; "punse his yed off," shouted a third party; and there was a general rush towards the gates, when the person before observed appeared at the bend of the lane, and advancing to the crowd, he made his way through them, and turning at the gates, he fronted the mob, before a word was spoken.

"What now? what will he say?" "hush! hush?" said others; and there was a dead silence, all the faces being turned towards the person.

"What is your business here to-day?" asked Mr. Staidley; for it was he.

"We want the loan of your hands, for a small job

we'er about," said the speaker on the hedge : joining in the laugh which followed.

" Then it is not me you want," said Mr. Staidley.

" No ! no ! " was the general answer.

" Nor my property, perhaps ? "

" No ! no ! " was again the reply.

" Why then do you come upon my premises in this hostile manner ? "

" Bekase we want the loan of your hands, as I towld you, sur ; " said the speaker.

" Where are my hands ? those who are present, let them come forward," shouted Mr. Staidley ; and a considerable number separated from the crowd, and stood in front of the gates, men and women, and youths of both sexes were intermingled, for the females would not go into the rear.

" I don't pretend to have so absolute a command over my workpeople as to be able to dispose of their services, either to you or any other persons," said Mr. Staidley, " but here they are, you can speak to them, and if they choose your employment rather than mine, I have not, as you see, any means for preventing them, even had I the will to do so."

" Speak out then, and tell us what you are about, and what it is you want," said one of Mr. Staidley's carders, to the mob leader.

" Well ! a dillicat meeting was held at a sartn place last night," said the hedge orator, " and it was determined to bring out all the hands until we get the owld prices. We were to begin with the hands at Downfasts, of Toilington, and then march to Brimbeck to get the people there out; and then wid go round and gain the whole counthry; and that's what we wants the hands at this place for."

"Well, my lads and lasses; you hear what they want you for," said Mr. Staidley, "will you enter their service, or remain in mine?" Speak out and tell your minds, whichever service you choose."

"For my part, I think it's only reasonable, what they want," said Ned Burfielt; whereupon there was a great shout, and cries of "hear him! hear him!" "I say I think it's only reasonable, because we here have our full wages, the same as they ask for, and it's only right that we should assist others in gettin their's."

"Bravo! bravo!" "good lad!" "fine fellow!" were vociferated, in compliment to the speaker; and, "Come along, let's be off, Brimbeck for ever, hurra! hurra!" were shouted by the crowd.

"Three cheers for the brave lads of Brimbeck," shouted the orator, taking off his hat and waving it; three loud cheers, and one cheer more, were given, with waving of hats in the air.

"I suppose you are all for liberty," said a light-haired, tall young fellow, who stood above the crowd opposite the fugleman.

"Oh, aye! liberty for ever!" shouted the mob.

"Three cheers for liberty, then;" said the young man.

"Now for liberty," said the fugleman; "hip, hip hurrah!" and the mob shouted for liberty.

"Very good," said the young man; "I'm glad to see that; now I, for one, shall take the liberty to go to my work inside the mill here."

"An' so will I," "an' so will I," "an' so will I," shouted a number of voices. "We'll all go that has a mind," cried out another.

"Aye, all that has a mind," cried most of the hands.

"Won't you abide the resolutions of the dillicat meetin?" said the fugleman.

"Who was the delegate for Brimbeck?" asked the young man.

"I don't know his name, but he stands there," said the leader, pointing to Ned Burfielt.

Ned seemed to shrink from this public recognition.

"And who appointed thee a delegate," asked the young man, accompanying the word thee, with a contemptuous and searching gaze. "Where, when, and by whom was thou appointed to act as a delegate for Brimbeck."

"Well," said Ned, putting the best face he could on the matter, "as the thing has come out in this way —though I don't think that Mister O' Flabberty, the speaker there, had a right to mention my name; but as it has come out—I'll tell the whole truth about it. A man whom I knew, came to my house on the night before last, and said, 'there was to be a delegate meeting, at the Three Wheels, at Toilington, and some person from Brimbeck was wanted to attend, and I might as well just go over and hear what was determined.' So I went to the meeting last night, after the mill was closed, and about half a dozen persons were there, and when they called over the names of places that sent delegates, there were none for Brimbeck only me, and I told 'em I was not regularly appointed, and O' Flabberty there, and all the rest of 'em said, ' pho ! pho ! what did it matter whether I was appointed or not, they would appoint me,' and so they put down my name for Brimbeck ; an' that was how I was made a delegate.''

Cheers and laughter followed this declaration, mingled with expressions of disapproval.

" And what did you do after you was made a delegate ?" asked the young man.

O' Flabberty protested against the question, as an attempt to " worm into the secrets of the trade," and to " upset the freedom of discussion ; " and there was a great uproar and noise in the mob ; whilst most of the workpeople stood laughing at the scene.

" Come," said the young man, " I will not be put down, I'm for freedom, you know ; tell us, Ned, what took place after you were made a delegate."

" Well," said Ned, " I will, I'll tell all ; " for he had begun to perceive that the hands were a strong party, and that besides those at the gates, there was at the end of the lane, another body of the mill-men with Jonathan Handy at their head, and he thought that some of them seemed to have short cudgels under their jackets :—" I will, I'll tell all about it," said Ned.

" Hear him ! hear him ! " shouted the young man, and the mill hands. " Down with the knobsticks ! " shouted O' Flabberty, and the shout was repeated by the mob.

" Liberty ! liberty !" cried the mill hands, " let the delegate speak," and in the end they prevailed, and Ned went on.

" Well ! O' Flabberty there, was chairman," said Ned, " and he made a speech, telling us, trade was getting worse, and workmen's wages lower. He said there was too much work in the market, and that the masters were tyrants, and ought to be resisted ; and then he talked gloriously about liberty, and freedom, and such like ; and he said some poetry about " Who so base as be a slave," and " Oppressions, woes, and pains," and such like, till he quite bothered me, and 1 believe most of the others were the same. Well, at last we agreed there should be a turn-out, and a collection ; and when the turn-out took place, the delegates should have five shillings a day, and meet every night, at some place ; and the chairman and secretary were to have three shillings a day extra, because, as they said, they would have to be " always at work for the good cause," and O' Flabberty was made into the chairman, and one Mc. Haggis, a north countryman, was appointed secretary, and——

" Oh ! the thraitor !" cried O' Flabberty ; " Down

with him! down with all knobsticks! all inimies of working men."

"Down with all enemies," shouted some of the mob, whilst others cried, "hear him! let him speak! go on, go on!"

"Well! after drawing up the rules, and signing our names as delegates," said Ned, "we left the Three Wheels, and went to a public house called, The Crib, where we found a number of Shuffleby's hands, and our chairman told 'em about the strike that was to take place, and that a number of mills were coming out, and they might as well join the others, and they seemed to like the plan. And he asked if they had not something in dispute about gas and the size of wheels? they said they had; and he said they might as well join in "the glorious struggle for their rights," and they said they would; and it was agreed to set persons to let the hands know as they went in this morning, about what was to be done, and that they were to turn out at breakfast time, and then go in a body, and call the other mills out, and that is all I know," said Ned.

"And enough too," said Dick O' Brella, looking fiercely at the men whom the leader had planted near him. "Enough too, be off, you humbugs and foos, and let honest men go to their work."

"Hold, Dick, hold," said Mr, Staidley; "be not so hard; recollect the people have been duped;" the remainder of his rebuke was unheard in the uproar which arose.

" Here's a knobstick," shouted one who had been planted to mark Dick. " A knobstick ! a knobstick ! down with Staidley and his knobsticks !" was shouted by the mob. O' Flabberty, the leader, promoting the tumult by his voice and gestures.

A stone was flung, and alighted near Mr. Staidley. " Ah ! you scoundrels," shouted the hands at the gates. " We'll not join you. Be off with your delegates ! we have our wages, and will keep 'em !"

The leader had disappeared from his elevated situation during the last tumult, and a voice and accent much like his, now shouted from amid the crowd, " Down with Staidley ! down with the gates." Others, who imperfectly heard the command, cried, " Down with the delegate," and a fellow who stood near Ned Burfielt, felled him to the ground, and others kicked him whilst there ; Ned bellowing most loudly, and crying for mercy. Meantime a rush forward was made by the mob, and a counter movement by the hands, brought the two parties into contact. Two fellows laid hold of Dick O' Brella, but he shook them from him with a bitter smile, and one went down with a blow, and the other with a kick that made the blood spirt. Half a dozen soon followed the others, for as the song of Grinfilt says, " He fought at both ends," and there was soon a clear space before him. The tall young fellow, before noticed, whose name was Alik O' Salls, also did considerable damage with his feet and hands. He made a ring for himself, and then cleared a passage towards his respected employer, whom he determined to defend with his life; a strong band was already around Mr. Staidley, and Alik took his place in the front, where he fought side by side with Dick O' Brella, and the mob was kept at a respectful distance. Several of the women also rushed out, and beat their bagging cans until they were flattened about the heads of the individuals whom they encountered, and numbers of the mob fell back, whilst others stood shaking their gory locks, and wiping their bloody faces unwilling to renew the contest.

" Stone 'em ;" shouted the same voice and accent as before, and immediately a shower of stones was hurled at the defending party; a charge which proved rather disastrous to them, for Dick O' Brella was knocked down by a blow on the mouth, and Alik O' Salls was floored by a like salute on the temple, which drew blood in abundance, and so probably saved his life; the mob then made another rush towards the gates, and there was a shout of " pull him eawt, deawn wi' him ;" and several of the mob attempted to lay hold of Mr. Staidley for that purpose, but his workpeople fought bravely, and soon rid him of his assailants. Meantime a great confusion took place amongst the rear party of the mob, who were supplying stones to the others. Jonathan Handy deemed it time that he and his men should go to work, which, as they were chiefly armed with sticks, he wished to avoid if possible, lest serious damage should ensue to some of the misguided multitude. He now, however, gave the word to set on, and in a moment, cudgels were playing as quick as batting sticks, on the shoulders and arms of the mob, and cries, curses, and tones of wonderment and pain, broke from the astonished and affrighted crowd, which separating, rushed through gates, and over gaps and fences, continuing their flight, in ludicrous and almost pitiable terror. A small party alone, unconscious of what had taken place behind, continued the attack at the gates; and these also, after getting a sound drubbing, which Mr. Staidley in vain endeavoured to prevent, were, at length kicked down the lane, and allowed to escape.

The gates of the mill were then opened; the wounded were taken care of; and Mr. Staidley, after exchanging friendly congratulations with his faithful workpeople, and giving all necessary directions to Mr. Handy, returned alone through the streets of the village, where he occasionally passed groups of the mob that still lingered drinking at the public houses; few of them however, then noticed him; they seemed ashamed, and dispirited, and he with a feeling rather of pity than of anger, went on his way towards home.

WALKS AMONGST THE WORKERS

No. VI.

TONGE AND CHADDERTON.

WORK FOR THE SCHOOLMASTER AND THE MISSIONARY.

In the lower, or southern part of the township of
Tonge, the extensive silk and cotton dye works of Mr.
Walter Beattie, are situated; near them is the newly
erected mill for the manufacture of silk smallwares and
ribbons, belonging to Messrs. Royle and Jackson; a
little to the north, at a place called " The Lodge," Mr.
Gill has a compact and well adapted concern for spinning and weaving cottons; at Spring Vale, a short
distance from this, is the malting concern, and the
brewery of ale and porter, belonging to Mr. Anson;
and, at " The Old Engine," near the railway station,
is the colliery of Messrs. Whitehead and Andrew; with
these exceptions, and a few others, such as farmers
and their labourers, bricksetters, joiners, blacksmiths,

and other individuals, all the population is employed in hand-loom weaving, either of silk or cotton.

Of the silk weavers it would scarcely be fair to draw a general inference from their present condition, as to employment. After a long season of full work, at steady wages, the silk weavers, like many other operatives, experienced, at the latter end of autumn, a sudden check in the stoppage of many of their looms. From the latter end of October to the beginning of February, in each year, there has generally been a greater or less want of employment amongst the weavers; this year it is more decided and of greater extent, and the distress among the poor is correspondingly increased, but there is nothing in the present state of employment which should lead us to suppose that it is anything more than one of those periodical depressions, caused by the annual pause in the market, which is affected by the seasons, and is, consequently, in a degree beyond the influence of human arrangement. In former years it has not been unusual for one-fourth or two-fifths of the weavers to be waiting for work, in the month of December; at present we shall probably be near the mark, if we say that three-fifths are waiting, or are under a tie not to bring their work in within less time than six weeks, which is equivalent to waiting one half their time. As to the average earnings in such a state of things, it cannot with reason be guessed at, nor is it required in the endeavour to approach fair general conclusions. In the best of times, there are here, as at other places, individuals and families who are " distressed "—who never were, nor ever will be, in any state, save the " distressed one." Others there are who are really distressed, but never make a song of it—who keep it to themselves, and, like good men and women, good fathers and mothers, meet hunger at their threshold, and, without whine or outcry, endeavour to repel it with all their energy. This is done every year by scores of individual families, and the world never hears of it; nor is it known beyond their own hearths, or, mayhap, those of some humane neighbours, not quite so poor as themselves. These sort of people have not leisure to go round talking of their " distress," nor would their pride let them. They are the sort that should be looked after by the ministers of religion, by the rich and beneficent, by the overseers of the poor; they should be *rescued*—they should be *sought out*, and comforted. I am sorry to have to express a belief that, at this particular time, there are amongst the working population of the above townships, and their neighbours also, many decent and really respectable families, who are struggling hard, and sinking daily— where the children become paler and thinner, and the parents more naked, stripping their apparel for a scanty dish of food; but this description cannot as yet, by any means, be applied to the bulk of the people. Their case is certainly *bad ;* but it is not like that of the operatives of Stockport and Bolton, *worse* after being a long time *bad*—not like a battle to be begun when the breath is already expended—a race maintained when it should have been terminated—a night continued when morning should have dawned. The depression here has come at the usual season, and though, as I have said, sudden and more extensive than in ordinary times, the good run of work which prevailed during spring, summer, and part of autumn, will, it may be hoped, enable the weavers to bear up until the trade of the new year shall put them again on their looms, with plenty of employment, good wages, and steady payments.

I know that I shall be blamed by some of the operatives for admitting thus far—for giving anything short of a picture of total distress. Exactly as, according to information, I was blamed at Heywood, for saying the workpeople were decently clad, and the children were cleanly and good looking; and as some persons at Royton condemned me because I had said the habitations of the factory hands at Crompton were kept in a cleanly and respectable condition. But the approval or condemnation of these persons, or, indeed, of any persons, unless well founded, cannot be suffered to interfere with a statement intended to express simply the *truth*, without reference either to individual likings, or the struggles of parties.

Of the mental condition of the population of Tonge, Chadderton, and their districts, some opinion may be formed after the recital of circumstances arising out of a late melancholy accident, (as is to be feared). From its perusal the christian may be urged to promote the spread of a wiser and a better light; the learned may trace the living follies in which his forefathers believed; the mere reader may be amused, and the narrator of christmas tales may have a subject for the fire-side group; and in any case we may learn how much remains undone towards the common-sense instruction, and the reclamation from error, of our own "benighted ones;" of the children, as it were, of our very households.

On the night of Sunday, the twelfth instant, Archibald Hilton, a decent, elderly man, sixty-one years of age, after attending as waiter to the company at the funeral of one of his early comrades, left the public house at Lower Tonge, where the funeral had been held, to go home to the hamlet of Jumbo, a distance of about a mile and a half from the public house. It was about ten o'clock at night, pitch dark, rather stormy, and as there had been a fall of rain that afternoon, the brooks and waters were considerably swollen. Hilton's direct road, however, did not lie across any water, but for a distance, not far from the edge of a stream called Wink's-brook, dividing the townships of Alkrington and Tonge, which brook, like all the others, was, at the time, swollen by the afternoon's rain. He was observed to be rather touched with liquor as he went out of the public house, and a person offered to accompany him part of the road, but he said he could do without assistance, and he went out, turning, as was supposed, in the right direction towards home, and from that time to the present day, (Wednesday, December 29th, 1841,) he has not been seen or heard of. He wore a black hat, a blue cloth coat, a checked cotton handkerchief round his neck, velveteen olive-coloured small clothes, strong shoes, had a tooth out in front of the upper jaw, and carried in his hand a blue cotton umbrella. For days all the brooks and waters, and pits, and every place where it was conceived he could possibly be concealed, were searched. His up-grown children and his neighbours, (he had no wife) were out late and early, making enquiries, and dragging and grappling for his body, and as the sons were one day engaged in the latter duty, one of their wives, attended by some neighbour women, came and proposed that "a cunning woman," living in one of the stone huts, near Collyhurst bridge, should be visited and consulted respecting the fate of the lost man, and the place where, if dead, the body might be found. The husband made light of the proposal, but one said the cunning woman had told one thing truly, another mentioned another proof of her wonderful knowledge, and they all set off to the house of the cunning woman, at Collyhurst bridge. Nine or ten persons were in the house when our inquirers arrived ; and, after waiting three hours, the daughter-in-law of the missing man was admitted to the presence of the prophetess. " What was her name ? " demanded the sybil. "Betty Hilton," replied the woman. "Was she christened Betty or Elizabeth?" asked the sybil. "Betty," was the reply. "Well," said the sybil, looking at a round glass, "you're come about a very decent, quiet old man, sixty-one years of age, and you're in great trouble about him, I see." "I am," said the woman. "But what's the meaning of this funeral?" said the sybil—"and him following after it?" Betty told her about the funeral the old man had been at, and that he was an intimate friend of the person buried. "What's the meaning," said the sybil, "of him going home?—I see him, and he turns down a narrow lane, and towards a water; and now a cloud comes over all, and I can see no more." "Was it a running water or a still water?" asked Betty, in the utmost simplicity. The witch said she could not tell, for the cloud prevented her seeing; it betokened death, and the man would never be found alive. She also said Betty must come over again; meantime she would "set a sign for him," and would "endeavour to trace him," and if they found him they must come or send her word as soon as it took place. They found him not; and the daughter-in-law went again, and the sybil then said she had endeavoured to trace him, and he was in water, not far from a white or light-coloured house, a cindered road, a dung heap, and a cart, with the shafts thrown up; those were signs as to the place where they would find the body. All these "signs" they found upon, or near the premises of Mr. Dudson, at

Rhodes, and close to the bank of the river Irk, of which Wink's-brook is a branch. They searched above and below, as well as at the place, several days, but neither the body of the missing man, nor anything appertaining to it, had they found at the above date. Other conjurors have also been visited by the relatives and friendly neighbours of Hilton. He was much respected, and a very general interest has been felt on his behalf; and some friends, who went to a " ruler of the stars," in Lord-street, Oldham, were informed by that adept, that the man was killed, either by a fall or a blow; that he lay in a hollow place where there were many stones, and that if he was in water, it must have come to the place and washed him away—he could not go to it, for, " there was no water planet ruling that day."

Numbers of the poor man's friends and acquaintances have sought the advice of one of these "Seers," who resides in Burnley-lane, near Oldham, which neighbourhood is rife with them, there being not fewer than seven in that vicinity. This man told a different tale from the others, and such was his plausibility and confidence, or assumed confidence in his predictions, that he was invited to the house where the family of the lost man resided. He went, and there was a very general examination and trial of his wonderful glass. A room was set apart for him up stairs; it was darkened from the outer light, and a table, a chair or two, and a burning candle, were placed for him. When a

o

person went in, which they did one at a time; he read a kind of incantation, calling on the heavenly spirits to lend aid and assistance in discovering the body of Archibald Hilton, who, to the great distress of certain relatives, &c., was lost. The person then looked through a pear-shaped glass; he was to look with a very steady gaze, and if, after some time, he did not see anything, the angels, Michael, Gabriel, and Raphael were invoked; and if the person still did not see anything, our Saviour, Jesus Christ, was called on to lend assistance;—the wizard would, at this last stage, place his hand on the neck of the gazer, who by this time would hardly fail to notice a black speck or specks, which seemed to be floating in the glass. When he announced these, he was directed to look more intensely, and after some time they would begin to enlarge, and probably assume something like the shape of a human being. These were pronounced to be the lost man, and the head stocks at Alkrington colliery, near to which place the conjurer declared the body to be lying. He even said the body would be found by eleven o'clock on a certain day, wisely adding, " or if not on that day, it would be found in nine days after."

The body was afterwards found in the river Irk, below the works of Messrs. Schwabe, at Rhodes, near Middleton.

AN INSANE GENIUS.

————————

JOHN COLLIER, commonly called Jacky Collier, one of the sons of Tim Bobbin, became insane, and died at Milnrow, near Rochdale, after having been for years an object of much interest and commisseration to all who knew him. His appearance was most striking, as he wore all his clothes the inside out, or the wrong side before. He was tall and bony in person; very grave in manner, and reserved in speech, and he generally carried a large stick, so that to persons who did not know him, he was as much an object of alarm as of attention. His coat buttoned behind, gave him a grotesque appearance, but the scowl of his eye, especially when annoyed, was sufficient to check all disposition to mirth at his expense. He seldom spoke, even in reply to questions; and, being harmless, except when exasperated by being interfered with, he was generally allowed to have his own way, and he led a silent life, wandering about the neighbourhood, entering such houses as he chose, and, when hungry, taking such food as was offered, but never asking for anything. He was an excellent draughtsman, and a good portrait painter ; and on such occasions, he would take up a piece of chalk or a pipe, and with a few strokes on the chimney-piece, or the hearth, he would give an admirable likeness of any person, or a sketch of any incident which took his attention. He had an almost constant pain in his head, and it would seem that he imagined his head was divided perpendicularly. His portrait, painted by himself, and lately, if not at present, in the possession of his son, is a very singular production, and a most correct likeness. He is represented wearing a cap, something like the tiara of a Jewish high priest. His face is divided by a gash down his right temple and cheek, whilst his forehead is bound with a strap, buckled, and a bandage, seemingly a hoop, passes across his face and his nose, as if to prevent his head from separating. He wears a kind of loose vest or cloak, with the collar in front, and his eye lowering from beneath his antique cap, has a strange and fearful expression. On the back of the picture appears an inscription, of which the following is a fac simile.

"John Collier, Esq. Pinx. fi thfe ANNO DOM 1785 ÆT ERR CON 45 REALL ETERNAL PPPPP UNIV IMMORT ET SupMAG NⱯ. NⱯ. NⱯ."

A TEMPERANCE ORATOR.

AT a time when the temperance movement was making a great sensation in Lancashire, a meeting was one night held in a room at Middleton, at which a new convert, known as " Owd Pee," stood up, and shaking his head, expressed himself as follows :

"¡Aye, aw kno yo expect'n summut fro Owd Pee, but aw shanno say mitch this toyme ; aw'l gi' yo' a reawnd when none o' theese tother speykers ar' heer. Awve bin a dhrunkart theese ten yer. Aw laaft mony o' suit o' clooas i'th' aleheawse nook ; aw laaft 'em bi three shurts ov o' day. (laughter, and cries of " well done owd lad ") Thur wur no rags for th' rag-mon at eawr heawse i' thoose days ; aw laaft 'em o' i'th' aleheawse-nook. (Laughter) Boseeyo they'st ha' no moor o' moine ; noather um nur thur byegles, moynd tat. (Roars of laughter, and cries of " that's reet owd Pee.") Aye ! aye ! they'rn reet enoof when they geet'n me amung 'em ; when they geet'n owd Pee to be a foo for 'em. They'rn ust to ha' mhe agate o' feyghtin, an' aw went wom scores o' toymes wi' th' skin off mhe back, an' o' stuck'n full o' sond un durt wi' rowlin oppoth greawnd; but aw tell yo' awst do so no moor. Why, aw tell yo' aw've had bi three good shurts ov o' day torn off mi back, an' aw bin sitch o' foo asto goo wom an' want another, bu mi wife had moor sense nor me, an' wudno' let mhe hav it.

One day aw're in a aleheawse nosso very far fro' this place, an' they wantud to ha' mhe agate, but aw wudno' stur, an' so at th' last, th' lonlort son, a yung felley, coom an' fot mhe a cleawt. Aw lookt at him, an' shak't mhe yed; in a whoile he coom agen an' gan mhe another seawse, an' wawkt tort th' frunt dur. Aw sed, "felley, iv theaw dus that agen aw'l byet-te." Well, in a whoile he coom agen an' fot mhe another good seawse o'th' yed, an' so aw at him an' beete him seawndly, afore thur byegles cud fly in an' ridd.

Another toyme, when aw're agate feyghtin, they took'n mhe new cloggs an' sett'n 'em oppoth foyer, an' when th' battle wur o'er, they gan 'em mhe to put on, an' aw put 'em on, an' th' rascots stood'n laighin' at mhe, for they brunt'n mhe feet, but aw gran an' abode, an' it wur mony a week afore Dan Moors cud get mhe stockin' feet eawt o'th' sore places. (Loud laughter.) Aye, yo' may laigh, but mind yo,' they'n ha' owd Pee no moor for a foo; aw'l noather taste ale nor spirits. Aw'd bwoth ale, rum, an' gin i'th heawse when aw gan o'er dhrinkin, but aw never tucht none on 'em sinn, nor aw winno doo. (Cheers.) Aw shanno' say mitch moor neaw, but aw'l gi' yo' a greadly blow eawt sum toyme elze when ther's none o' theese tother speykers to tawk to yo'. (Cries of good lad Pee! well done, Pee! until he sat down.)

A PASSAGE OF MY LATER YEARS.

On the evening of a Friday in the summer of 1826, when so much damage was done by mobs breaking machinery, in the neighbourhoods of Blackburn, Burnley, Haslingden, and Bury; when many thousands of pounds worth of property was destroyed by the starving hand-loom weavers, many lives were lost, many of the aggressors were imprisoned, and many transported to die in foreign lands; it was, as I said, on the evening of a Friday of this eventful time, that a young fellow whom I knew, came to my house at Middleton—called me aside—and expressed concern at a plot which he said was being carried on in our vicinity. At first he seemed rather unwilling to disclose all that he knew, but after a little urging on my part, he said that certain persons residing in the neighbourhood, had been in the habit of holding secret meetings, and had once or twice sent delegates to the disturbed districts in the moors, inviting the loom-breakers to come down into our part of the country, when they would be joined by the working population, and might make a clear sweep of the obnoxious machinery, all round by Heywood, Middleton, and Oldham, and so return to their hills before any force could intercept them. I did not at first place entire faith in the representations of my visitant, and I told him I thought he must have been somewhat misinformed, for I could not fully believe that any parties in our neighbourhood would be so wicked, or were so mad as to encourage such a thing. He however assured me he was right, and he mentioned persons, and times and places of their meeting, which convinced me there must be some devilish scheme going on to disturb the peace of our hitherto tranquil district, and to cause a recurrence of scenes like those which took place in the spring of the year 1812, when sad havock was committed on property, and a number of lives were lost in our town; I therefore thanked him, and, as the only reward I could give him, promised to make some good use of the information he had afforded; and on further enquiries in certain quarters, I ascertained, that from a dozen to a score of persons of the worst character had got up the plot; that they had met secretly, and delegates, and messages had passed to and fro betwixt them and the leaders of the outbreak in the moors, and that the following Monday morning was appointed for their next meeting on the hills, when they would come down, and being joined by the workmen in our part, would destroy all the mill machinery that lay in their power.

I was, I must confess, even after all my experience with respect to popular commotions, somewhat startled at the blindness and audacity of this scheme; yet, that it would be attempted, I had no more doubt than I had of my existence, and I therefore determined to use my best endeavours towards preventing the attempt from taking place. I informed several of my acquaintance of the circumstance, and I even went to Manchester and made it known to the late editor of the Guardian, and having so far satisfied my conscience, I took upon myself the performance of the remainder of my purpose.

It happened at that week's end, that I was particularly short of money, so I went and borrowed a few shillings from one of my acquaintance, telling him what I wanted the money for. Another acquaintance, as poor as myself, had offered to pledge his watch to raise the money, but I declined his offer, being desirous of trying all other means rather than put him to such an inconvenience. Well, being thus furnished with the needful, I set out from home early on the Sunday morning, and traversing with quick and lengthened strides, the Parson's meadow, I ascended the high ground on the west of Middleton, leaving the wood—for there then was a wood—on my left, and Ebors on my right, I soon passed Langley hall, and went through Birch, and up Whittle-lane, and on through Pilsworth and Heap-fold, and so to Bury-moor-side. From this place, without stopping, I pursued my course until calling at a little shop, I quenched my thirst, and allayed my hunger by a draught of good sharp treacle beer, and a roll of gingerbread, and so went on to Edenfield, and thence to Haslingden, where resided a friend whom I believed had the power to assist me in my undertaking. I found him out soon after I entered the village, and having sent for him to a public house, I ascertained that he was the very man I stood in need of, and I urged him to introduce me to some of the leaders of the late outrages, that I might make known to them the deception that had been practised towards them in our part of the country, and the destruction that awaited them and their followers, if they ventured down into the low districts.

After discoursing some time, and partaking the refreshment of ale and tobacco, my friend agreed to conduct me to the parties I was in quest of, and we accordingly went out at the west side of the village, and after some time got upon the high moors, and to a place called Black Moss, where several persons were informed as to the nature of my business, and whither we were going. From hence we crossed a valley, and again ascended high ground, and at length stopped near a small fold of low stone houses, in a very lonely spot. My conductor left me, and entered one of these habitations, whilst I took a survey of the bold and lovely country around where I stood. On my right was Black Moss, the place we had come through, and, a little more in front was Humbledon, a hill where several insurrectionary meetings had been held. Beyond Humbledon, arose the smoke of Burnley, and before me was Padiham with its lovely valley, and its spectre-like population of weavers. Behind Padiham and Burnley, Pendle-forest stretched wide and far, with its sunny slopes and lonely dwellings, and its uplands thirsty with long drought, and its watered dells still verdant. Then dark Old Pendle lay huge and bare, like a leviathan reposing amid billows; whilst sweeping towards the left, stretched other hills and moors, to me unknown, but all dotted with houses, and marked by stone walls, and dark shadowy chasms, and green nooks, and wreaths of white vapour rising for miles and miles, and spreading on the wind. For, in consequence of the long drought, and the intense heat of that summer, the moors and moss lands had cracked into wide fissures, the edges of which had taken fire, and they were burning and smouldering in some directions as far as the eye could reach. Such is the recollection of the not unsublime picture of that bold and striking land, the abode at that time of a population reduced to famine and despair.

I had scarcely made such hasty survey, ere my conductor came forth, accompanied by a number of men, to whom he introduced me, and by whom I was received with a cold civility, not, as I thought, unmarked by tokens of suspicion. They were all decent, thoughtful looking men, and though the ghastliness of want was on their features, and though their clothing was poor, very poor indeed, there was nothing like either filth or squalor to be seen about them; their humble garments were neatly darned or patched, and their calico shirts were clean; it was Sunday, and they had don'd their best attire. Such were a group of Englishmen, of English Saxons in truth, fathers of families, living on two-pence halfpenny a day; how as many un-Unglishmen—of the finest pisantry for instance—would have born like misfortune, I leave others to describe.

We formed a kind of little meeting at a short distance from the houses, and as we conversed, others occasionally drew towards us, and joined us from different parts of the country. My conductor told them who I was, and where I came from; " that I had been in several prisons for seeking parliamentary reform; that I was at Peterloo, and was tried with Hunt at York, and being one of those found guilty, I was confined during twelve months in the Castle at Lincoln; that consequently I was an acknowledged advocate for freedom, and the poor man's rights, and understanding I had something of importance to communicate to them, he thought it his duty to bring me amongst them;" in short, he did me justice in a neat and brief address.

One of them asked if he knew I was the same person, the same Samuel Bamford he had been speaking about? and he said he did know me to be such; he had known me from a boy.

My identity having been thus established, a considerable portion of coldness seemed to have left them, and they asked what it was that I had to speak about?

I said I understood that delegates had been sent to them by parties in the neighbourhood of Middleton, and they said there had been a delegate up several times.

I said I understood that such delegate invited them to go down to Middleton to break machinery, and had represented the people in that part, as ready to join and assist them whenever they came, and they said it was so.

I said I believed the delegate's name was —— and they said that was the man.

I then told them that he was a discharged soldier, and one of the worst of characters; that those who had sent him were only about a score in number, and were all of them persons in whom no confidence was placed by those who knew them; that the people at large, and the reformers in particular, knew nothing of the plot, nor would they countenance it; that weavers at Middleton could get their eight or ten shillings a week, and I asked whether if they could do the same, they would not prefer to stay at home with their honest earnings, rather than turn out and incur the risks and anxieties which all outlaws and proscribed men had to suffer? and they all declared, some of them most earnestly, that if they could make their earnings anything like what the Middleton weavers got, they would never attend another meeting of an illegal character.

I then asked them whether it was at all likely that the weavers in our part would leave their good work, and their quiet homes, and their comparative plenty, to join in a thing which would deprive them of all their household comforts?—whether, if they themselves would not join in such a thing, it was likely the Middleton people would join in it? and they declared it was not likely; it was not to be expected.

I then conjured them not to be led astray by the parties who had been corresponding with them. I told them the men who had invited them would be the first to betray them, if they came down; and I urged them by every argument that occurred to me, to abandon their project and give up their mischievous connexion with the delegate and those who sent him. I said I had nothing in view in coming amongst them, save their own good; that after being made acquainted with what was going on, I should have considered myself a betrayer, if I had not come up and laid the whole truth before them; that I was not paid for coming; but did it at my own expense, and on my own responsibility; that I sought no reward save the approbation of my own conscience, and that, having thus performed my duty, the result must be left with themselves.

They all seemed grateful for the interest I had taken in their welfare, and informed me that a meeting had been appointed at an early hour on the following morning, for the purpose of going down to Middleton, and that they would have gone down ; but that, in consequence of my coming up, they would inform the meeting of what I had stated, and leave it then to be decided upon. I urged them not to omit doing this, and they promised they would not ; and so reminding them, that if they now came into our part, they would do so with their eyes open, and with the sin and the responsibility on their own heads alone, I and my guide took a friendly leave of the men, and returned to Haslingden, from whence in a short time, I set off towards home, and arrived there at night-fall, having travelled about thirty-six miles.

Well ! the following morning betimes, the little knot of villains who had concocted the business on our side of the country, were on the alert, and listening until their ears cracked, for the sound of an uproar, and an approaching tumult, but nothing was heard.

They sent scouts up to Ebors, to survey the hills of Birkle and Ashworth, and to return and report when they saw the multitudes pouring down towards Heywood, and they went up, but all was still, and not a sound was heard ; the chimnies were smoking, and the factories working at Heywood as usual ; the hill-sides lay mapped out in the clear air ; the white kine were seen browsing, the new washed linen was seen bleaching in the sun, and the whole country was as quiet as on any other Monday morning. This was perfect consternation to the plotters. Well ! eight o'clock, ten o'clock, noon came, and there was no change; nothing was heard save the report of cannon down in the S. W. and that was soon ascertained to arise from the practising of some flying artillery, who, with cavalry, were traversing the road betwixt Bury and Manchester, so that the troops, it would seem were also on the alert. The day thus passed over in tiresome watchings and vain expectations, and when night came they were informed by one of their own messengers, a swift footman, that according to the appointment, a large meeting assembled that morning, at Humbledon, expecting to make the promised descent, but that several of the leaders were averse to it, and in giving their reasons for being so, stated all I had told them on the Sunday, and added other reasons of their own, arising from what I had said; the consequence was, that there was a complete division in the meeting; some from towards Blackburn, Padiham, and Burnley, were still for proceeding, whilst those with whom I had conversed were decided not to do so, and a third party seeing these divisions, entirely withdrew. The meeting therefore broke up without coming to any effective determination; the thing fell through, the plot was frustrated, and it never again was revived.

Happy was I that morning, when looking over my little garden. I was startled by the reports of artillery; happy was I when having learned that troops were on the Bury road, I reflected that but for me, that powder, instead of being wasted in parade, would

P

probably have been expended in the sacrifice of human life; and the happiness arising from that reflection has been my reward.

On the other hand, the disappointed plotters, who only wanted an opportunity to plunder, were ferocious against me. Several hole and corner meetings were held, at which I was denounced as a spy and a traitor; at one of such gatherings held in a chamber at Bury, I was voted to be a fit subject for assassination; but I never could learn that either the proposer or seconder undertook to complete their resolution. To my family these things were annoying, but I treated them with contempt. I did not even go out with a stouter cudgel than usual.

It was just at the expiration of a month from the time when this plot was defeated that another of the sort was developed, and promptly put down; it lasted long enough, however, to confirm what I had said to the poor calico weavers on the moors, as to what would be their fate if they came down, and depended on the co-operation of the weavers at Middleton; it exactly bore me out in all I had stated, namely, that those who had invited them would be the first to betray.

At eleven o'clock on a Saturday night, about a hundred and fifty, or two hundred strange men, from towards Manchester, most of them armed, entered the market-place, at Middleton, and called on the people to turn out and bring their pikes. They stood there drawn up in line, and repeatedly shouted for their Middleton friends to come and join them. Not a soul responded to their call, and they began swearing, and cursing those who had ordered them to come. At length they began leaving their ranks, and some of them went into provision shops, and others into public houses, and demanded refreshment. This had just begun, when a furious clatter was heard; a party of dragoons came galloping up, and the invaders disappeared as totally as if such things had not stood in the place. It was like a scene of enchantment, and the inhabitants who witnessed it were quite bewildered. Several of the fellows, however, were taken and put into the lock-ups, and the persons most active in their apprehension, were of that very class of operatives from which they seemed to expect assistance.

The plot on the moors having been frustrated, it was renewed thus, and with more effect amongst the hand weavers of St. George's Road, Little Ireland, and other out districts of Manchester, and we have seen the result. The fact was, the originators were a set of thieves, who wished ro get up a row, that, during the scuffle, they might plunder the more securely. Both attempts as we have seen, failed, and I count it not one of the least fortunate circumstances of my life, that I had so large a share in the frustration of the wicked and cowardly schemes of those worst enemies to society.

WALKS AMONGST THE WORKERS.

No. VII.

MIDDLETON AND TONGE.

HAVING last week glanced at the condition of the hand-loom weavers of Tonge, and part of Chadderton, it can scarcely be expected that those of Middleton should not have a similar notice bestowed on them. The course of work is nearly the same in all the three townships; the number out of employ may be reckoned the same, viz: three-fifths of the whole number of the hand-loom weavers, and the ratio of distress— distress of some families, and serious embarrassment of others—is also about the same. Since my last communication, I have conversed with a most respectable gentleman, who has visited a district in Middleton which is supposed to be the worst conditioned of any in the town. He bears out my views with respect to the actual state of the working population; and says that, though many families are really distressed, the distress is not so entirely unmitigated as he has reason for believing it is in some parts of the country; it has not yet come to a stripping of the beds and the denuding of the walls of the houses for the procurement of food. In fact, as I had stated last week, the distress has come here after a good season for work,—I might have said two good seasons—and the people were in some degree prepared for it. To the general evil of want of work, there are, however, some relieving exceptions. The extensive concern of Messrs. Salis Schwabe and Co., of Rhodes, who employ, on an average, from six to seven hundred hands, are—with the exception of their block printers—all in full employ, and more than that, for most of the workmen make very long over-hours, and they consequently draw a handsome little sum at pay-day. The spinning and weaving concern of Messrs. John Burton and Son is also in constant work, as is that of Mr. Gill, at The Lodge; whilst the small-ware manufactory of Messrs. Jackson and Royle, at Lower Tonge, which employs about one hundred hands, one-third of them perhaps being females, is, like Schwabe and Co's., exceedingly brisk, and the hands are encouraged to do as much over-work as they can. These concerns, as may be inferred, embrace a considerable number of the population, and keep them at work, leaving the evil to rest, as before intimated, upon the hand-loom weavers, and some others dependent on that branch. Messrs. Stone and Kemp, an extensive firm in London, having a silk manufactory at Middleton, are, like others in the same branch, slack of work at present; and their weavers feel the pressure of the times. The superintendent here is, however, as I am informed, in the habit of affording relief in food to some of the poor weavers; Messrs. Schwabe, of Rhodes, do the same, not only by their own short-working block-printers, but the distressed from other parts: the principal of this firm has also given a sum of money for distribution to the poor in the town of Middleton. A gentleman, connected by property, and recently dwelling in the neighbourhood, has likewise sent ten pounds to be distributed; a munificent lady in an adjoining township, has also been very good to the poor, visiting them at their houses, and relieving their wants with her own hands. Nor, I am gratified to have to say, must I stop at the clergy of the establishment; without mentioning names, or clerical distinctions, which, I believe, they would rather avoid, I feel bound to say that they have done, and are still doing all they can, in visiting, inspecting, and relieving real objects of charity, without reference to creeds in religion, or parties in politics. Besides gifts from their own resources, and they have not been either small or few, they have become the almoners of others' bounty, and the poor have hitherto, and probably will continue to be, both cared for and looked after. It is further, as I understand, in contemplation to get up a concert in the course of the present month, the proceeds of which are intended to be given to the poor. The churchwarden has also, this Christmas, made his annual distribution in cloth, to the amount of about sixteen pounds; so that, on the whole, by the time the spring trade comes round, the weavers will have an opportunity for returning to their work, with their hearts imbued with one of the most pleasing of sentiments,—that of gratitude.

The styles of work done here are from the commonest *gros de naples*, up through printed work scarfs, tippets, satins, and jacquard work of all descriptions, besides the smallware silks done at Messrs. Jackson and Royle's, some of which are also woven by jacquard. There are abundance of hands, most of them familiar with silk from their infancy; coal is cheap, water plentiful, ground-rent low, rates very light, and roads (beside the Manchester and Leeds railroad) good; carriage being, consequently, easy and cheap, there is a fine opening for the establishment of manufactories by one or more London houses in addition to that of Stone and Kemp. The wages are below those given in London; for instance, *gros de naple*, three thousand three hundred reed, are fourpence per yard; satins, six thousand reed, seven-pence three farthings; six thousand four hundred, eight-pence farthing; satin shawls, seven-fourths, four shillings and sixpence each, and the same, eight-fourths, five shillings and sixpence. Last year these shawls were each a shilling more for weaving; but they have been reduced, it being allowed that they would bear a reduction better than any other article in the trade. The shawl manufacture has been most dull here within the last three months; it is expected, however, to revive in a few weeks, as preparations are in progress by several houses for an increase of that article. It is probably expected that the reduction in price will tend towards increasing the demand. One house, in Manchester, is working a variety of goods by the steam-loom; the weavers receiving two shillings a day, and it is said that one of these looms will turn out two shawls a day. This is certainly bringing things to the lowest cost at once, so far as workmen are concerned; but how it will work in the gross, at Manchester, where chief-rent, rates of every description, coal, and other outgoings are high, is best known to the parties trying the experiment. Another house, I have been informed, is removing its crape-weaving from the district of Chadderton, and is about weaving it in town, in a place prepared, and by steam. If these experiments answer, in a few years the fate of the calico hand-loom weavers will have become that of the silk hand-loom weavers—a fate which they are not all expecting, nor in the least prepared for. But whether the work is to be done by hand or steam, Middleton offers about the finest field for the experiment; and, if I might hazard an opinion as to the result, I should say that, when our provision laws shall have been relaxed or done away with, and other measures of free trade introduced, the hand weaver will beat the steam weaver whether he will or no; a

result which the holders of large weaving establishments little expect.

In the higher parts of the township of Tonge many
looms were, some three or four years since, employed
in weaving broad cotton table cloths; numbers of
these looms are now occupied with a description of
carpets for the foreign market, that of South America,
and a rather fanciful description of cotton scarfs for
personal attire.   There is room for an increase in
these last articles, and, indeed, a probability that both
these and the other courses I have mentioned will
continue and increase, notwithstanding experiments in
machinery.

WHAT SHOULD BE DONE?

Friend Acreland,

You put me in mind of my implied promise to recur to the above subject, and I take the present opportunity for doing so.

You know that we agree, or at least, I assume for argument's sake, that we agree with the declarations of government, and the ministers of religion of nearly all denominations, that, " the people should be educated." But we go further than do either the state ministers or the religious ministers; we say the people should, nay must be fed and clothed before they can be educated; and in order to this, they must be employed, and paid for their emyloyment. Not the off and on employment which is the frequent lot of too many of our workmen, but constant employment, such as will bring its Sunday dinner and Sunday duds with every Sunday, and its good substantial meal with every meal-time on the working days. I mean to say that whenever a man works, or wherever he works, he should eat his fill at meals; and that no man who can work and is willing to do so, and thereby to earn his bread, should be prevented from so doing; if he is prevented, there is something wrong somewhere. This may suffice to show what I mean by being employed and fed.

Now then, how is that grand panacea, employment, to be procured? I say, unfetter commerce, promote agriculture, and leave the rest to heaven and our own long heads and hard hands, and fear not. Unbind the swathed giant, Industry, and see if he won't assume a multiform that shall keep both want and the world at bay. Yes, unfetter commerce; abolish the duties on food; cease to make land dear, bread dear, and, at the same time, labour cheap; in short, extend to commerce the principle of your improved postage, and depend upon it, similar benefits will follow. Whatever is lost in the price of things, will be more than made good by increased demand, and prompt payment; and thus there would be more labour, more food, and, no doubt, plenty of both.

"Oh, Oh!" methinks I hear you say, "you're coming on with your free trade jargon now; couldn't you argue the question without touching that irritating subject?"

The question, friend Acreland, is, "What should be done?" and I am stating my views as to what should be done, together, in my humble way, with my reasons for those views.

You know I am in principle a free trader; you must have known it long, for you cannot have forgotten my telling you, and repeating it to others in your hearing, how I was one of those who went to the great meeting at Manchester, in 1819, and that on one of our banners were inscribed the words, "No Corn Laws." You have heard me declare that all the reforms we asked for on that day, I would still obtain if I could, or modifications of them fully equivalent to what they would accomplish in the way of reform. This matter therefore is settled. I am a free trader from principle, not from expediency. I advocated it when it was dangerous and disreputable even in this town of Manchester to do so, and I still advocate it; because, in the first place, it would increase employment and make it constant; it would increase food, and make it cheap, and doing so, it would tend to make the people more happy, more tranquil in their minds, and more susceptible of that cultivation which I deem to be absolutely necessary to the permanence of government, and the welfare of the people.

But though these are strong reasons why I should be an advocate for trade, and a free trade in corn especially, still stronger reasons, have all along, presented themselves to my mind. Many good men here, in this South Lancashire of ours, are opposed to the corn laws, because, as they say, and I believe truly— they injure trade, and restrain manufactures. These, considering our present state of society, are also strong reasons against the continuance of those laws, but I am moreover opposed to them because they are wicked; because they are an astounding evil to mankind; because they snatch the crumb from the lips of the hungry and toil-worn, saying, demon-like, "not yet; thou hast worked for thy bread, now work for the tax ere thou eat it;" "thou hast worked like a good man for thyself and thy children, now work for the squire's extra rent; work for his dog-kennel, and his daughter's portion, and his lady's jointure, and his son's outfit in the world; work now for these, and then take thy loaf and eat." Well, the work is again set about; but, whilst it is being performed, what else is going on in that man's heart? why deepest hatred to be sure! rebellion is born! vengeance is laid in store! infernal machines are planned! plug-drawings are dreamt of! rick-burnings are meditated! and a general havock, and an up-setting, and a down-casting, and a wide wasting of life and property, are looked to, and hoped for, as the only cure for a burden so intolerably unjust, and audaciously oppressive. Yes, it is because the corn laws are eminently wicked that I am opposed to them. A bad trade is a woeful bad thing for this country, but it is nothing compared with the curse of living under laws which we daily and hourly execrate because of their injustice. Hunger, we know, will "break through stone walls," it is so hard to endure; it kills the body, it murders by inches, or rather by crumbs; but hard work though it be thus to kill the body, is it not harder to kill the soul ? to put to death God's image in the heart ? to cast forth all mercy and kindness, and patience, and beauty; to thrust these away, and to fill their place with hatred, cruelty, rapine and overt revenge, all working bodily peril and pain, and soul-damnation. Is not this harder ? is it not a deeper sin ? Then comes the demagogue to make a fermentation—a kind of hell-bubble of all these passions and things; and fitting dupes, ready-made dupes, oppression-stamped dupes, finds he waiting at hand. One shall have " a great demonstration," another " a sacred month," another " a charter," a fourth " a fire-light meeting," a fifth prefers " lucifer matches and a homestead," whilst a sixth shall be most handy with his " knitting needles, amongst the cog-wheels," and a seventh, wisely advised, and implicitly obeying, shall, " draw from his bank, and lay out his children's coffin and shroud money in the purchase of pike, and dagger, and gun, and pitch-torch." Such instruments have unjust laws prepared for the hireling demagogue, and the cowardly instigator.

Still I have not done; there are deeper thoughts to come out yet; and if you, dear Acreland, have any acquaintance either with Sir Robert, or the Duke of Richmond, you may just let them know all I tell you. I have not any secrets in these matters Turn-about Chartists and their present employers, may affect to know better than I do, but never mind what they affect, confide in what I say, and be assured that men's thoughts are taking a deeper turn than either the Duke or Sir Robert are aware of. I have seen the people when discussing in groupes by the road-side,—or the field walks—by the hedge-nooks—on Sunday mornings— far from the League and all its influences—in the sweet balmy air of summer—amid the sun-showers of spring —on the cold eve of winter—and after the day's work in autumn—I have seen them in various situations, and under many different circumstances when expatiating upon, and denouncing the corn laws. I have seen them with their brows knitted like cable ropes, and their eyes flashing, and their strong arms stiffened, and their fists clenched as hard as mallets, by the influence of indignant emotion caused by this great wrong. I have seen these outward and visible signs of their inward feelings, and I have also heard words which made my ears tingle, and my heart leap; words that coming from the quarter they did, and elicited under the circumstances they were, I knew to be ominous of no good to those who, despite of all warning, of all entreaty, continue these bad laws.

" If ever the time does come,"—I have heard it said,—" and that it will come, is as sure as that yon sun will set in the heavens; if ever the time does come, when the whole people shall assume their rights, and shall discuss their claim to the whole land; whenever that time arrives, the strongest argument for the measure; the strongest charge against the landowners will be the fact of their having whilst in power, enacted

a law to keep up rents ! to make bread dear ! to fill
their own pockets at the expense of the rest of the
community ! Ah ! the short-sighted ones ! why not
mete out to us the breath of heaven ? why not charge
us with our sun-light ? why not gauge and tax our
wells, and our brook-steads, and rock-springs. Why
not ? for these are not more our inviolable rights, our
absolute necessaries, than is the bread for which we
have toiled. The injustice cannot continue ! it cries to
heaven ! it disquiets the earth ! and assuredly it will
cause a just, but a terrible retribution. Will not our
children say in those days ? and shall we instruct them
otherwise ? will they not say, " Let this landowning
class cease. They were entrusted with power and they
abused it ; they were endowed with honour, and they
disgraced it ; they were endowed with riches, and they
remained sordid ; they were exalted amongst men, and
yet grovelled with the lowest ; they might have been
merciful, but they were cruel ; they might have been
munificent, but they were avaricious—mean ; they
might have been just, but they were unjust ; they
might have learned wisdom, but they preferred ignorance ; away with them ! they have been weighed in
the balance, and have been found wanting ; they have
had their day ! Our fathers and ourselves have long
since paid for the land by unjust taxation, and we
will have it ! away with these fellows ! the land is ours !
put them out ! down with them ! "

Such, friend Acreland, is one of the results of unjust

laws : one wrong begets another ; one outrage lays the foundation—sanctions the perpetration of more extensive outrages ; and though the bread-tax has become a law, it is not the less an outrage against common sense, and plain common right.

Away then, I say, with the corn laws, and all other laws that tend to make food, or clothing, or house, or land dear ; abolish them as speedily as possible.   Let the people be employed ; let the people be fed ; let them be comfortably housed ; let them have all bodily necessaries for their labour ; set their minds so far at ease ; let their hearts be ameliorated ; cultivate their generous feelings ; let contentment and thankfulness be awakened ; then instruct their minds, and teach them all useful knowledge suited to their capacities and pursuits.   Let the ministers of religion give their aid, and eschewing—if it be possible they can learn so much charity—creeds and dogmas, let them agree upon and teach the broad essentials of christianity ; keeping the husky, worthless disputations to themselves, who have time for those things.   Let this be done, and we will soon have a cultivated people.

Such a people would not be long in obtaining, by fair, by peaceable, by honourable means, all the civil rights they wanted.   The labouring population would be what it ought to be, at once the support and defence of the state ; the middle class would transfuse a vigorous life and action, and thought, through all the body politic; whilst the monied and landed class—no man then wishing either " to put them down," or " thrust them out "—would live in security, like elder brothers, or fathers of a happy and grateful household. England, aye, and Scotland too, would thus have their rights; would have justice, and having got it, wouldn't wait long ere they took care that Ireland should have it also; yes, there would be " justice for Ireland" then you may depend upon it, friend Acreland; justice for Ireland in full. Irishmen would then cease to bluster and blarney—neither having much effect with us— they would then become more just towards each other —a thing they are sadly in want of, on that side the water. Then we would strip Paddy of his rags, and his filth, and flinging them to the devil—if we could— we would clothe him anew, and bring him home like a brother that had been lost too long. We would seat him at a board as plenteous as our own, and thus with all kind treatment, we would put into his head better things than he has learned from his priests; more noble sentiments than those he heard at Mullahmast and Tara. This is what we "Saxons," would do, and do it also, not because we cared one rush about any repeal hubbub that might be going on; not because we deigned to bestow even one pitying, pshaw! on the bullyism of Yankee and Mounseer, put together, but because we Saxons having obtained our rights, would wish to see our neighbour Celts have theirs also; because, that strong feeling which impelled us to become free ourselves, would not let us be happy until, from the uttermost verge of our state, should be heard the voice of a free, happy, and industrious people.

I am, dear Acreland,

Your's truly,

SAMUEL BAMFORD.

Blackley, July 16th, 1844.

TO THE EDITOR OF THE MANCHESTER ADVERTISER.

Sir,

Will you allow me a short space for a few words in reference to the conduct of the persons styling themselves chartists, at the meeting held for the repeal of the corn laws on Friday last? Of all the political inconsistencies which have come under my notice, none has appeared to me more unreasonably and humiliatingly absurd than were their proceedings on the above-mentioned occasion. A number of poor, and some of them personally hard working men, are heard to complain of oppression, and they adduce as a proof of it, the raggedness and famine to which themselves and their class are subjected; yet they clamour, not *for*, as one might expect they would, but *against* cheap bread! which, in fact, means cheap everything, —cheap clothing, cheap rent, and cheap government, in its degree.

Twenty-years ago such a thing would have aroused universal indignation throughout the ranks of reform. The old fathers and dames of those days—the wives and children, would scarcely have credited their ears, if told that in any part of the kingdom a body of working men had been found who not only repudiated a petition for abundance of bread for themselves and families, but actually insulted and abused others who were endeavouring to obtain it for them. Major Cartwright, Lord Cochrane, Sir Francis Burdett, William Cobbett, Henry Hunt, and all the leaders of reform, would have denounced the " famine-seekers " at once, and would have declared their proceedings treason against the first law of nature, and blasphemy against the first prayer, " Give us this day our daily bread," and a long and deep groan of execration would have arisen from the toiling and hungered myriads from one end of the island to the other.

One of the most offensive banners which appeared at the great meeting of the sixteenth of August, 1819, was that whereon was inscribed " no corn laws," and at nearly every reform meeting throughout the kingdom resolutions were passed condemnatory of the corn laws. Seldom were those obnoxious statutes forgotten. But now the chartists say, " we won't have cheap bread, unless we have the whole charter also ;" which is equivalent to saying, " we won't have to-day's dinner until to-morrow's breakfast is ready,"—" we won't have our meals at three separate times, but take them all at once,"—" we won't wear jackets until we get clogs," " we won't, in short, accept any part of all that we want ; we will have the *whole* or nothing."

Was such a thing ever propounded by sane minds before ? Is there in all nature any known power to enable poor imperfect man to rise instanter, of his own will, a perfectly endowed being ? In all time, has such a feat been accomplished by individual, or multitude, or nation ? In all history, does such a record occur ? If God himself was six days in perfecting creation, why should not erring and feeble man be content to work out whatever he may seek for good, with such humble means, and by such protracted labours as his imperfect condition and acquirements impose upon him ? recollecting, as he should, that he has not only to struggle against his own weaknesses, but against those of other fellow creatures, who may be as much disposed, and certainly have as great a right as himself, to close their ears against the truth, or to shut their eyes against the light.

The slave who refused nourishment until he died or were free, would act consistently and so far respectably ; but one who said, in mock heroic, " Well, if I must remain in bondage, I'll be up with 'em at any rate—I'll make my life as extra miserable as I can—I won't eat a belly full of meat, hang me if I will," he would only get laughed at, whilst his experiment would assuredly break down in time. About eighty years ago, a poor weakling, known as Know-man, used each Christmas to visit the old Assheton family, at Middleton Hall, on which occasion he generally had a silver sixpence given him as a present. At one time a gentleman who was on a visit would give him a sixpence also, but Know-man, shaking his head and looking cunningly, said, "Nawe, nawe, I'll ha' no fresh customers." The chartists do the same, they will " ha' no fresh customers," " no fresh aids." They may be sensible men, I don't dispute it; but poor Know-man was always afterwards set down as unfeignedly crazed.

Even in our commonest transactions, how thoughtful we must be, and how carefully we must move, step by step, in order to secure good and escape evil. What thoughts and schemes from night to morn rapidly succeed each other, ere we advance one good day, nay one good hour in life. And yet a party are found who tell us we must obtain all our political rights at once, or accept nothing. What would our country chartists think if Robin O' Dick's, or John O' Tummie's, or any other of our great Lancashire apple or gooseberry growers, were to stand by his trees, and refuse to gather his fruit as nature offered it, declaring he would have none until the whole were ripe, until one grand shake would bring the whole down? Would they not turn away seriously, and say when they got home, that so and so was utterly demented, and that the overseer should be fetched, and the poor fellow should have a blister on his head? Would they not say so? To be sure they would, and speak sensibly and humanely too. Yet such is the system which the chartists avow and boast of.

Why, is not the whole of man's life made up of a multitude of little events and things, following each other as fast as ourselves and nature can force them? Is not our existence a succession of stages of being, until we are, step by step, matured in our several degrees? Do not our mothers, and our fathers, and our own recollections attest this to us? And do not we attest it to our children? Is there any other possible way, save the step by step one, in which we can work to our meridian and end? Is it not consistent with all nature, in everything? Are not our houses set up brick by brick? And our wells dug spade by spade? And our trees hewed with many blows? And our ships floated after many stages of preparation? Yet, in politics, we are told, we must jump to a conclusion! —we must have a miracle!—a perfection all at once! We must get up some morn, "lords of the creation," indeed! or we *will*, and our wives and children *shall*, remain ragged, starved, and moody slaves!

In all science, Englishmen may be accounted as proficient, at least, as those of any other country. In the science of politics (the forbidden one) they are, as I believe, with the rest of their species, as yet but children, comparatively: but because "an Irish gentleman" has chosen to recommend that they at once attempt a master-stroke in the science with which they are the least acquainted, the experiment must be tried! a miracle must be wrought! the "charter of democracy" must be obtained in the lump! Well! who'll go into the stronghold of the withholders and fetch it out? Several have sworn aforetime they would,—but did they do it? did they keep their oath? Poor John Frost was the only one who kept his word,—who did more than talk. He raised the devil about his ears,—but what laid him? The blood of the poor vain man's comrades, and the sacrificing and dungeoning of his better-hearted dupes.

Oh, no! the chartists may depend upon it, that if they will go forward to erect a monument of patriotism, they must proceed in a regular, cool, and workmanlike manner, as good workmen always do. They must take the best materials they can find, and use them to the best advantage, forming the mis-shapen, and softening and bending the stubborn with much patience and skill. It will not do to get ill-tempered and sulky, because all they want is not ready fitted to their hands; they must not bluster when the winds blow, nor stand haranguing when the waves roar. No Demosthenizing! there has been too much of that; no bragging about rearings and "goose-eatings at Michaelmas;" no swagger; that don't make bricks. They must work patiently, and steadily, and permanently, and wisely, and the more silently the better. They must, in short, begin with a beginning which I fear they don't like to try; and until they do so, there can be no hopes of a good end.—I am, sir, your obedient servant,

March 24th, 1841.   SAMUEL BAMFORD.

WALKS AMONGST THE WORKERS.

No. VIII.

TOWNSHIP OF BLACKLEY.

THE township of Blackley is divided from that of Alkrington on the north by a narrow stream, which runs from the White Moss on the east, and passing Alkrington Green, enters a deep woody vale, and joins the Irk, near Rhodes, on the west. This woody vale is accessible by a sloping road which diverges from the turnpike road at Alkrington toll-gate, crosses a culvert over the stream, and turns to the right. Then, proceeding along its margin on one hand, with high meadows and a rude fence of hazles and hedge-wood on the other, presently enters a sequestered dell, shrouded by tall young timber, the brook on the right, other timber and high-grounds beyond, and a row of yew trees fringing a bank on which stands an ancient thatched dwelling, with another yew tree before the door, and a barn at the eastern end. Passing beneath the dark branches of the yews, a very pleasant field walk stretches along a narrow valley, the little stream still accompanying us, and the high-grounds of Blackley skirting our left, as the wood of Alkrington does our right, until we emerge in a fine broad meadow, with the waters and pastures of Rhodes before us, stretching towards Middleton, and one or two genteel looking residences in front. With this sketch of the valley in our eye, let us revert to the top of the glen, and commence our progress from the yew trees. Standing here, and looking towards the Alkrington side, we observe part of a cottage and a modern small mansion, embowered in the wood; these, together with the estate, are the property of Dorning Rasbottom, Esq., who came into possession on the death of the last of the male line of the old proprietors, Darcy Lever, Esq.; whilst the little freehold on which we stand is the property of the occupier, Mr. Taylor, whose family employ their time in farming and domestic manufactures, but, "the humble shrub remains unbroken, whilst the strong oak is uptorn and destroyed." From this place a narrow old-looking lane guides our steps up a steep bank, and towards the south, in the direction of the village of Blackley, in the township of which we are already.

Still ascending the lane, we soon come to two houses, one of which is occupied by a small farmer, and the other by a family of weavers. Two women— an elderly one winding bobbins, and a younger one with a child on her lap—are sitting by the fire, and, in answer to my questions, they readily shew me the loom-shop, and describe their domestic condition. One loom contains plain printed gros-de-Naples, three thousand reed, at fourpence per yard; and the young woman should weave six yards of it per day, but she complains it is bad, spoiled in the stamping, and much of the warp comes off broken. This I can believe, from the excessive carelessness I have myself noticed in the processes both of dressing and printing. Such carelessness is a cause of great loss both to the weaver and employer; to the former, in the additional labour which it causes, and to the latter, in the deteriorated quality of work which results from it. Probably the weaver in this case would not be able to produce more than four yards of cloth per day, which would come to one shilling and fourpence,—or eight shillings per week. The other loom contains a reed of common check, cotton warp, and part of the woof, or weft, linen; this is seven-eigths in width, and fifty-four yards of it—a good week's work—come to four shillings and sixpence, or a penny per yard; winding, dressing, paste, and all outgoings included. This is, one would suppose, low enough in all conscience, but last year it was worse, being then seventy yards for five shillings and sixpence,—or seventy yards for sixty-six pence. In another loom was a gingham, five shuttles, sixty yards for eleven shillings, of which, probably, with hard work, the weaver would earn seven shillings; so that here four persons (one being gone out, and not counting the child) with weekly earnings of nineteen shillings and sixpence,—or four shillings and ten-pence half-penny a week each. The rent of the house was five pounds, the rates would probably be about six shillings a year, and their coal a shilling a week at least—say for the whole three shillings a week, or nine-pence each; they would then have four shillings and three halfpence each to purchase food, clothing, and to supply every other contingency. But there was no outward sign of distress here, nor any great demonstration of discontent. The woman, to be sure, wished things were better—thought they had not enough for their work, and I thought the same; but there was nothing like squalor, or dirt, or shiftless thriftless despair about them or their little cot. The walls and the floors were clean, the windows whole and shining, the place was decorated with maps and pictures of fierce battles, Lady Godivia riding through Coventry, and other antiquated and legendary subjects, but all seemed cleanly and cheerful, and the one woman with her babe, and the other with her wheel, seemed disposed to make most of the homely enjoyment of their own hearths, upon which burned a good coal fire.

A little further on the side of the lane stood a cold, genteel-looking house; the gates, doors, and shutters of the place were all closed, and it looked just as cheerless and forbidding as an English built house could be made to appear. A man, apparently on business, stood outside the yard gate, which he could just look over. I asked why he did not go in, and he said there were great dogs within that would tear him in pieces. I said I would go round to the front door if I was him; and he replied the dogs could go there also, and he had no chance but to wait till a servant came; and then he set up a whistle! At a short distance further I stood before a low brick lodge, at the gates of spacious grounds connected with an elegant, but uninhabited mansion. On a board over the door of the lodge was a notice that "steel traps and spring-guns were set on the grounds." Even here was "machinery!" these, not to feed the hungry, or clothe the naked, or to find them employment, but to cause cruel hazard of life, and manglement of limb! Strange that a vastly rich, and certainly charitable and good young lady—as the last resident was—keeping here her maiden state, should have permitted such a "raw head and bloody bones" notice to terrify old women from gathering sticks, or children from going to the wild dell for primroses! Separated from this great and now voiceless mansion by a shrubbery only, stood another desolated dwelling, of humbler pretension certainly, and screened from the great house by the trees, as a lady would lower her parasol on one side to prevent her from noticing a humble acquaintance. This was, a short time ago, a small farm house. The wife brought her husband a fortune of a few hundreds of pounds; he settled himself and family here, and was in a fair way for doing prosperously. But reverses came; his good wife died; his farming went to rack; he tried to make a stand by earnings from the loom; those also, from some cause, were insufficient; and he commenced the illicit trade of distilling and selling whiskey. He was informed against—the excise seized his still, and carried off all he had on the premises, leaving his children (for he had fled) the bare flags to sleep upon. He returned into the country, was taken, and is now a prisoner in one of the gaols of the county. The windows of the house part were now all beaten or blown out; the grates had been pulled down; the floors were broken up and scattered over with rubbish and dust, and where the voice of an affectionate mother had, not long since, been heard caressing or admonishing her young ones, now all was silent, save the moaning of the wind, the flapping of casements, or the creaking of doors.

At Crab-lane-head, which is a small hamlet of weavers, I found them chiefly employed on linen drills, a kind of strong cloth, cotton warp, and linen weft, used for trousers; plain and striped nankeens; gingham; and common blue and white checks; their earnings on which, would vary, supposing health and constant work, from eight shillings to four shillings per week. Where there was a family of active weavers they would, of course, be in decent condition; and where it was otherwise there would be found distress; in fact, the wages of cotton weavers are down at the lowest possible rate on which they can earn a poor scanty diet ; those earnings cannot be reduced without sending them in shoals to the Board of Guardians. In the village of Blackley are a number of check weavers, and their earnings are about the same as those stated. At Charlestown are one or two silk weavers; the remainder being employed on cotton. Two old men were at work in one shop, one of them working at a furniture check, at six shillings and sixpence a cut, admitted he could almost work one in a week ; he was a very active, hale, and cheerful old man. He said " he was young," he was only born in the year 1766, and was consequently, only in the seventy-seventh year of his age ! His fellow workman was weaving a cotton stripe ; he was very cheerful and good looking for his age, though I thought a little more tardy in his motions than his fellow labourer. " I am older than that," said he, smiling. " Why, how old are you ? " I asked, and he said, as he stood leaning against the fire-side, " I am in my eighty-sixth year ! " Their united ages would, therefore, amount to one hundred and sixty-three years. The house in which they lived seemed poverty-stricken and neglected ; a sickly woman was in the place. The old men were both cheerful, and cleanly, and apparently healthy. I saw them both at work in one shop, the " young one " dressing and the other weaving. I did not ask their names, but they live in the highest house of the left hand row, going from Blackley village. I have only to add, that with a few exceptions, the dwellings of the poor at Crab-lane seemed to be in neat order. Many had white or coloured shades to their windows. The avenues around their cottages and outward premises were in good order, and gardens with clustering fruit trees, gave an air of rural economy which was pleasing to notice. Many of the residents in and about the village of Blackley, were out of work, in consequence of the stoppage of a large printing and dyeing concern, and of two others working short time. I am convinced, however, that the labouring population of our country will never submit to habits of burglary, until every honest mode of subsistence has been tried and found wanting. Woe to those then, who, for any pretence, make this industrious poor into brawling mendicants. Such a population as ours,

" When once destroyed, can never be supplied."

MOST IMPORTANT QUESTIONS.

" He (Mr. Marshall) inquired how tenants were to pay their rents, and how landlords were to live ! "

TO THE EDITOR OF THE MANCHESTER GUARDIAN.

SIR,

The above questions form the concluding sentence of a paragraph which appeared in your paper of the twenty-sixth ultimo, and they were stated to have been put by Mr. Marshall, a magistrate, residing, I believe, in the northern division of the county, at the annual session, held, as I suppose, at the Court House, in Preston.

Mr. Marshall having, in some observations which preceded these questions, referred to my work, " Passages in the Life of a Radical," with some part or parts of which he seemed to coincide, I think I shall not be presuming too much if I tender, by way of replication to Mr. Marshall's queries, such opinions on the subjects propounded, as my share of experience and attention have enabled me to form. I shall therefore be much obliged if you will allow me space in your valuable columns for this purpose; and I should be well rewarded, could I persuade Mr. Marshall, or any of his friends, or his party (understanding him to be a tory,) to adopt my views on the matters under consideration.

To the first question, " how are tenants to pay their rents ?" I reply, they are not to pay their rents, that is, their present rents. It is of no use mincing words: we had best be candid at once, and make ourselves understood. They are not to pay their present rents—rents must come down. They were advanced enormously during the long war, and the paper-money times; and now Peel has brought us back to metal money, which has decreased wages and prices, why, rent must e'en follow, and that for one very good reason alone, out of many, they can't be got, and therefore they can't be paid. Peel's metal money bill gave to high rents, and to all artificial prices, the first blow ; and his tariff bill has given the second. He has hit the monopolists all around him, right and left, and pretty hard too : he has, whether wittingly or not, done good service to the nation.

I would not wish the landed interest to be pulled down, I would not even have it humbled in reality ; I would certainly wish the class to have less money,

the same as other people are having, but they should
have plenty of the good things of this world for it.
The manufacturers will let them have cheap goods, if
they would let the manufacturers have cheap bread;
and when food and clothing are cheap, I defy pride,
or luxury, or bad government, to keep other necessaries dear. I would not have one of them worse off,
according to his rank, than was Sir Raphe Assheton,
the last male of the ancient house of Middleton. He
lived like a king amongst his tenants, and was beloved
like a father. I have heard old people say, that his
tenants and poor neighbours would have eaten every
mouthful of the earth which covered him in his grave,
if by so doing, they could have restored him to life
again. He was the last of that sort, as well as of that
name. We have since had lords, but none so noble-
minded as old Sir Raphe. He was munificent; he
kept up the ancient customs of hospitality; he comforted the poor, and was blest where'er he went; he
drew his money from his tenants, and he spent it
amongst them; he did not go rambling and gambling to
London, Paris, and the —— knows where; he was an
old English gentleman, a kind neighbour to every one,
and a protector of his neighbours. I should like to
have seen the squad of chartists that would have dared
to say, " turn out," to any of his men. Yet this rural
king, this comparatively poor, but really great man,
did not receive as much rent from the whole township
of Thornham, as is now paid for one farm only in that

township. If I am rightly informed, and I have it
from a pretty sure source, his rental for that estate did
not amount to one hundred and fifty pounds a year;
yet he lived in plenty and honour, and what more
could the most selfish aristocrat desire?

I have before me an old manuscript, purporting to
be, " A terrier of ye glebe lands and other possessions,
appertaining to ye rectory of Middleton, as the same
was surveyed ye sixteenth day of September, Anno
Dom. 1663, by Robert Symonds, rector, and ye
churchwardens." And from it I extract literally the
following entries, viz :—

" First, Isaac Walkden, one dwelling house, of five
    bays, in outhouseing two bays, one croft of one rood
    land, one garden of ye yearly rent of five shillings,
    and in boons yearly one day shearing, and one hen,
    and an hariot at ye death and decease of every tenant
    or tenant's widow of ye premises."

" Richard Hilton, one dwelling house of two bays, one
    barn of two bays, and one garden, upon ye yearly
    rent of one shilling ; in boon one day shearing, one
    hen and hariot, *ut supra.*"

The above, it would appear, were cottages; next comes
    a farm :—

" Jonathan Jacques, one dwelling house of four bays,
    one barn three bays, other outhouseing two bays,
    one garden, and twenty-eight acres of land by esti-
    mation or yr about, and in boons yearly leading

five load of turfes, one day shearing, one hen and an hariot; at ye yearly rent of eighteen shillings."

Such were the rates at which cottages and farms were let under the rector of Middleton, in the year 1663. The rents are now, of course, a great deal higher; though I don't believe they are let at more than a fair valuation as land goes. To the aforesaid state of things we should endeavour to approximate; and the sooner we begin to retrace our steps, the better.

To the second question, " How are the landlords to live?" I say, live as Sir Raphe Assheton did. Live with your tenants, and more *for* them than it has been your wont to do during the last fifty years. Come back to the halls of your fathers; build up " your old waste places;" renew the fires on your ancient hearths; call around you kindred hearts for the same goodly purpose. Such may yet be found.—Surely all the noble emotions have not become extinct. Cast an eye of mercy on the poor—encourage the good—repress the evil. If you call yourselves " conservatives," be such in reality—in action as well as in word. Be, indeed, " repairers of the breach;" " restorers of the paths to dwell in." Your ladies, also, may find plenty of suitable employment, and pleasurable too, for their leisure hours. There are such acts of mercy as administering to the wants of the sick, relieving their distresses—(our Saxon mothers got their title by that) —throwing crumbs of instruction in the way of the ignorant and unthrifty of their own sex, and in holding up the fainting hearts of the sensitive and hardly used. They might do all this, and more, without soiling their delicate hands, or sweeping the hovel floors with their costly garments; and I am sure their hearts would be the easier and better, and their looks more lovely, for having done it.

When the good old knight I have mentioned used to come home from the chase, he brought with him the poor hungry lads who had been hunting all day,—he brought those as well as the rich. The lads were placed in the great hall, around the huge fire; and there, whilst the knight was with the gentlemen in the parlour, the pedestrians were plentifully regaled with beef, bread, and good brown ale. He did not "cut their company" when the day's toil was over, and leave them to go swilling bodily and mental poison at the hush-shop, nor to ravage turnip or potatoe fields to satisfy hunger. He treated them so that he could meet them as humble friends another day; and he sent them home singing like throstles in a morning. This is the way in which they should live. If gentlemen would be honoured, let them act with honour, and they shall have their reward.

But if the landlord ask, " How shall we pay our taxes ?" Oh, the taxes must come down also, and the manufacturers will help you to accomplish that. There must be a general retrenchment of the public expenditure, the burdens must be more equally laid on, and the fundholder must carry his share. Yes, when once rents have given way fairly, the landholders will all be for cheap living; they will join the manufacturers, and will become thorough free traders. Conservators they may remain of useful institutions; but they will certainly be reformers of abuses, and curtailers of lavish expenditure.

How, then, is this desirable change to be effected? How are the landlords to be convinced of their error? By the same means which convinced the manufacturers of their error. The latter never, as a body, became sensible of the necessity of a free trade in corn until the ground began to shake under them—until their capital was in danger of being swallowed up. This is an undeniable fact. When the Radicals went to Peterloo, to petition for the repeal of the corn laws, —as all true radicals, both now and then, would do,— where were the great men of the league? why, they were either banded with the tories, or were just " nowhere," as regarded that question. But times began to get bad, trade decreased, profits were reduced; and then, like men true and sensible to their own interests,—as all men will be more or less,—they looked at the thing, and became repealers. The same cause will produce the same effect, wherever it operates. Sir Robert, and the inevitable circumstances which are hounding at his back, will, must, nay, have already, begun a reduction of rents; receipts will become less; expenditures will be reduced; no class will be exempt;

there will be a shaking down of feathers from the high roosting places, as well as in the road-side nests. Much false pride will be dropped with the false plumage; and a more sober mode, both of thought and action, will pervade all classes.

Meantime, I would say to the manufacturers, "Be a little patient; take the good advice Mr. Hindley offered you the other day; go forth instructing, but not exasperating; conciliating, not denouncing; bear a little; consider how recent has been your conversion; recollect it was but as yestermorn you awoke in tremor; give others a little time to rub their eyes; and depend upon it, the very same cause which so unpleasantly aroused you, will awaken others ere many suns have arisen and gone down. One good stagger in the rent market, and it reels a little now, will make the landlords spring from their lair, and send them scampering over to you, with a whoop, and a holloa, that will ring through all Downing-street.

That voice arose with the radicals; the manufacturers, after a long interval, have taken up the echo; the chartists (shame and contempt to their name!) have opposed it; the rural tenantry will revive it; their masters will hear it; decreased rents will make them understand it; their mistresses will feel it in the clipping of useless pride and luxury; it will become a topic for anxious discussion in the higher circles; parliament will reiterate it in a voice which allows not of any mistake ; a low fixed duty may then be proposed, but eventually the corn-laws will be repealed, and it will then be seen what can be done to restore the prosperity of England.

I am, sir, your obliged,

SAMUEL BAMFORD.

Middleton, November 1st, 1842.

A STRANGER IN LANCASHIRE.

A conversation, of which the following is the substance, once took place betwixt a stranger, a pedestrian
traveller, supposed to be Sir George Head, during
his "Tour in the Manufacturing Districts;" and a
resident of Moor-side, near Littleborough. Persons
acquainted with the general character of the population
of that part of the country, will recognize in the in-
quisitiveness, the superstition, and the simplicity of
this countryman, a correct portraiture of the manners
of a Lancashire peasant, manufacturer, and farmer of
the present day. When Sir George Head stood to
see the pigs washed at Huddersfield,* he spent his
time to no better advantage than he did in listening to
the sharp turns, and broad credulities of this lone
dweller of the moor-borders.

The scene is near a stone cottage, with a porch whi-
tened inside, and a tall elm spreading its branches
above the roof; a barn and shippon are in the same

* See his "Tour in the Manufacturing Districts."

inclosure, and the whole are situated on the top of a green slope, on the edge of a dark and cheerless moor. At the end of the cottage is a rock spout, from which, sparkling like dew-pearls, a rindle of water tumbles into a stone trough. A bare-headed, dark-eyed, and ruddy-brown damsel is washing in the shade of the tree; the master of the house, a man some forty years of age—with a slouched hat, a greasy blue jacket, a striped woollen apron, twisted round his waist, ribbed fustian breeches, brown stockings, and clogs on his feet—is calling back his cur Twitcher, which is dodging the heels of a gentleman coming up the flagged foot-path towards the cottage. The stranger after the usual compliments, says,

" Pray, can you inform me which is the nearest way to Littleborough?"

"Wot, dun yo myen past th' Chanters, at th' Lone-foote?"

" I do not know where I should go past, sir."

"Oh! yo dunno' know, dun yo? but I'll goo wi' yo, an' show yo. See yo then, yo mun goo deawn th' Little-feelt, an' deawn th' Yeaw-bonk, an' streight deawn th' Wood, an' yo'n soon be at th' Littleborough. Wot, aryo sum mack ov a wool-felley, or summut?"

Stranger.—" No sir; I am not in trade."

" Why, I thought yo hadn bin. Why, we'er dun yo come fro, then?"

" I come from London."

" Fro Lunnun, dun yo?"

Stranger.—" I do."

" Dun yo know Peel, then ? "

Stranger.—" Which Peel ? "

" Why, Peel at belungs to this lond."

" I am not aware that I do."

" Why, but he lives i' Lunnun ! "

" In what part of the town does he reside ? "

" Th' teawn ! he never lift i' Ratchda in his lyve, mon."

" I mean in what part of London does he live ? "

" Nay, I know nowt obeawt tat, but he lives i' Lunnun ; he's my lonlort, mon ; an' Cleggs-wood, an' owd Joe's too, belung'n to him."

Stranger.—" Then you hold this farm, I suppose ? "

" Ay ! ay mon, I live heer, but I'm beawn to lyev it : it's so deer, mon ; an' theers so 'ternal mony witches obeawt heer, too, mon."

Stranger.—" Indeed ! "

" Ay, thur is, mon. When I coom to this farm at furst, I cudno' churn, au' so I went to yon chap 'at lives at th' edge o'th' moor yon ; an' I towd him ; an he show'd me in a glass hooa it wur 'at did it. Seeyo' th' wizart lives at yon owd heawse wi'th' ash-tree at th' end ; an' so, when wee churnt th' next time, I put a red wot link i'th' churn,—an' at that same time th' owd devil wur so ill brunt, at it very nee kilt him ;— an' ever sin then, we con churn yezzy enoof. But th' barn's witcht, so 'at no mon con reer a cawve int'. I've seen 'em plump run op th' sides o'th' barn wall, like hey-goo-mad, an' then in obeawt a week afther, they'n begin o bein ill, an' they deen. Hanyo ony witches i' Lunnun ?"

Stranger, smiling.—" Not that I am aware of."

" Well then, yo'r weel off, heawever ; but I bin afther th' Turner yon, weer Robin lift ; dunno' yo know him 'at belungs to th' Turner ?"

Stranger.—" I believe I do not."

" Why, but he lives i' Lunnun too. Has he never towd yo 'at th' Turner, an' th' Sheep-bonk, an' a dyel o' farms obeawt heer belung'n him ?"

Stranger.—" No one has told me that."

" Why then, yo noather known him nor Peel ?"

" I do not. But pray now, what do you and your family work at ?"

" Why I weave flannel, an' th' wife spins for meh ; an' th' lads an' lasses weav'n cally."

" And how much may you have for weaving a yard of calico ?"

" A yard, mon ! they'n so mitch a cut."

" And how many yards are there in a cut ?"

" Why, theer's thirty yards i'th' Smithy-nook cal' ; an' they gett'n fro a shillin to eighteen-pence a cut : that at a shilling 'll be nowt a yard ! will it neaw ?"

Stranger.—It will not be much, indeed !"

" Mitch indeed ! ittle be nowt, an' nowt elze, mon ; that's plump."

Stranger.—" What business do you consider to be going the best in this neighbourhood ?"

" Why printin to be sure;—calico printin—it tells
for itsel, dusno' it ?   Look at yon felley at th' How-
side; when he coom a livin to this part at furst, hee'r
not so mitch better off nor his neybours; then he wed
a lass fro th' Hondle Hoe, an' bigg'd yon fine heawse
amung th' trees; an' then he started o' printin; an'
neaw he prints two theawsun pieces a week, an' gets a
shillin o' cleer profit o' every piece."

Stranger.—" That must be a good trade indeed !
but how do you know he has that profit ?"

" Why becose Tum o' Neds, o' Bills, o' Sally's,
towd meh so; an' beside I know it's true an' nowt
elze, for meh feyther has lift oppo th' Cawbrook o' his
lyve, an' he sesso; an' it's like to be true, isno' it ?"

The stranger turned aside and smiled, and said, " he
was sorry he did not hear so good an account of other
branches of manufacture, but he hoped they would
soon improve."

" Aye, theese great men op at Lunnun—said
Yethert—o' tawk'n o' that way, but it never happens
to be so; they reckont 'at Reform wud set o' things
reet—but by —— he's a great while i' comin, an' they
gett'n wur every day."

The stranger laughed outright at the notion of Reform being a person, and then said he must be going,
but before starting off, he asked the name of a small
fold of houses nearly opposite, but a considerable distance from where they were standing.

"Oh! they coan that, Th' Whittaker; Isaac o' Lee's lives teer; dunno' yo know Isaac?"

Stranger.—"I do not."

"Why that's quere, for he lives oppo his own lond: an' mistriss Lort, 'at lives o' this side o' Ratchda has two farms theer; dunno' yo know hur?"

Stranger.—"I do not."

"Why then, I'll be sunken iv yo known onybody, oather heer or at Lunnun. But afore yo gwon, I'll tell yo'th' road agen. Yo mun goo streight past th' Chanters, an' deawn yon Little-feelt, and deawn th' Yeaw-bonk, an' through th' Wood, an' o'er th' Yells-bridge, an' past James o' Sladin's, an' eawt th' road, an' yo'n soon be at th' Littleborough."

WALKS AMONGST THE WORKERS.

No. IX.

ROCHDALE.

The bright sun, like that of an April day, the exhilarating air, and the cool and untainted breeze, having tempted me to the heights of Castleton, I once more beheld the fair valley of the Roch, now mantled in snow, and made up my mind, at the moment, to bend my steps through a portion of that interesting district, which had so greatly attracted my notice the first time I went over Thornham, to observe the condition of the working population on the northern side of the hill. In coming to these fine breezy eminences, I had passed on my right, Royle, probably from the Welsh or Celtic, Ar Haul, pronounced Ar Hoyle, and Maydin on my left, another place with a Celtic name. Below, the little stream called Trows, crosses beneath the highway, and on the verge of it, in a small fold of cottages, stands the public-house immortalized by that rare genius of his times, and still more rare as to

s

place, Tim Bobbin. It was here the misfortunes of poor *Tummus* commenced, his calf being killed by " a tit," which stood at the door. So much for my transit hither, and some of the places worthy of notice on the way. Threading very pleasantly several of these old lanes, (beautiful strolling places in the spring time of life,) I dropped into the valley at a small hamlet to the east of Rochdale, and at but a short distance from the verge of the borough, and here entering one of the dwellings, I was presently welcomed to the fireside, and a free conversation with the occupant quickly ensued.

From general observations, the conversation soon turned to more direct ones on trade, and then to still more interesting ones on employment in the flannel manufacture, wages, machinery, and the domestic condition of the work-people. My friend (for so I will call him) was and is a respectable man in his sphere of life. He is a flannel weaver, and has followed that employment from his earliest years. He is about fifty-five years of age, and, with the assistance of his wife, who died about two years since, he brought up a young family in decency, and the enjoyment of a comfortable homely plenty. He is a person of more than ordinary observation and intelligence in worldly matters; is a Reformer, though not of the destructive school, in politics; a tolerant Christian in religion, a loyal subject to the Queen and the laws, and a " live-and-let-live " neighbour with all ranks. Having said thus much, it

will not be supposed that I can add anything to the
force and good sense of his observations; and I will,
therefore, so far as they are available for public purposes, give them in his own words. But, first, we will
have a description of the residence of the worthy
working man. The door and front windows looked
eastward; the space inside was about seven yards by
eight; the fire-place on the left of the entrance, and a
good oaken chest of drawers, with prints and draw-
ings in glazed frames, were on the right; a good oaken
couch chair, with specimens of needlework, and other
pictures, was fronting the window; and several bright
and neat seats were in various places round the house.
Over head was a bread-flake, but with a few oat-cakes on
it; some bundles of dried herbs, &c., but no bacon, ham,
or beef were seen. Opposite the door was a flight of stairs
to the chambers, and a passage leading to the cellar,
and to a small parlour, used as a bed-room; and on
the other side of the house was a small recess used as
a kitchen. The floors, the walls, and the furniture,
were all thoroughly clean. The chambers above, of
two heights, were the same size as the house; and it
should be remarked, that flannel weavers require capa-
cious, open rooms, on account of the space necessary
for their jennies, their working mills, looms, and other
implements of manufacture. At the head of the stairs,
in the first chamber, was a good bed in an old-fashioned
black oaken bedstead. Near that was a loom, at which
the weaver sat, tying in his work. Beyond the loom

was another decent-looking bed in an old bedstead; next that was a warping mill, taking up much room; then a stove, with a fire burning,—and then another loom. The looms each contained flannel work, of a fineness called thirty-two reed—such as is used for linings, petticoats, and other personal wear. The room was comfortably warm, and the arrangements were of that primitive and homely cast which reminded me of the free distribution of a Dutch interior; such is a characteristic of most of the working and sleeping chambers of the flannel weavers in the neighbourhood of Rochdale. In the upper room were two other jennies, of seventy spindles each, a loom, a stove, a bed, and other matters. Over head the naked timbers of the roof, and the cold unlofted slates. A clever, good-looking young woman, the youngest daughter of the occupant, was here at work, spinning wool on her jenny. His family consisted of himself, his son, and three daughters; all grown up, and unmarried. The weavers were, himself, his son, and a journeyman, who lived with another family. The young women spun the wool from slubbings, warped the warps, and did the house-work: and such were the domestic and working apparatus and arrangements of my friend's household.

He said things were very bad—not so much from want of work as from low wages; a master might reduce or abate at any time, and the weaver, in reality, never knew what his wages were until he had drawn them. The weaver brought the wool ready slubbed from the warehouse, and he spun it, warped, scoured, sized, beamed, tyed, and wove it; taking the slubbings back in cloth. The warp was made from lamb's wool, mixed with a little skin wool—that is, wool taken from the hide after the sheep is dead, as is that which the fell-mongers sell; the woof, or weft, was made from broke or shorn wool, mixed with a little skin-wool, and some foreign. The flannels he made were in the thirty-two reed, two pieces in a breadth, of thirty-seven inches each; the pieces were forty-eight yards in length, and the two contained forty-three pounds of slubbings. He brought the work from the warehouse, as before stated, and took it home when finished; and the whole was eight days work of twelve hours, and came to twenty shillings, to divide betwixt the spinner and weaver, or one shilling and three-pence per day each. His journeyman weaver had nine shillings and sixpence for each warp, and ten shillings, if he scoured and sized the warp himself. The house he dwelt in was his own, having been left him by his wife's father; if he had rent to pay he could not pay it, as things were now going. The rent and all rates, for such a house as his, would be about ten pounds a year; and his coals, having three fires in the winter, would come to about two shillings a week, reckoning by the year round. The rent, fire, and rates, we may say, would amount to fifteen pounds per annum, or two pound ten shillings each person; which would leave them about thirteen-pence farthing per day to subsist upon, and provide clothing, and all other necessary articles.

In 1824-25 he drew five guineas for work which would now only bring him two pounds; about twelve or eighteen months ago wages were reduced two shillings and sixpence in the pound, and there had been a gradual reduction, though at intervals, during the last sixteen or seventeen years. When he had six children, and the oldest only eight years of age, he could lay in a winter's stock of potatoes, and pay for them when he had them; he used also to buy eight or ten score weight of pork, and a round of beef to hang against christmas; ale he took when he had a mind, but always had plenty of it at christmas, for his family's use, and to treat friends if they came. He generally bought a tub of butter at once, and it was very seldom that he purchased *part* of a cheese. Meal and flour he laid in by the pack weight, and seldom purchased less during nearly thirty years in succession. When his children began to work he saved money, and was doing well, but the unions sprung up (the weavers' unions) and interfered betwixt the manufacturers and the body of weavers, and did much harm, He blamed the proceedings of the unionists, and was much abused at the time for not going with them in all their extravagancies, but they had since found out that he was right. The proceedings of the unionists, in collecting shuttles and destroying machinery, did away with all the old kindly feelings which had existed betwixt the employers and the employed. More machinery was then quickly introduced, and it had continued, and had been gradually extending ever since; and now, he believed, the manufacturers cared but little about the welfare of their workmen, but considered it almost a kindness to let them have a little work to do at their own homes. Things, in fact, were much altered for the worse, in nearly every way as it regarded the workmen. As it respected himself, he was now embarrassed on every hand; he had to contract small debts to keep his head, as it were, out of the water; he kept paying them off as fast as he could, but whilst he cleared one away he was getting fast with another. He now bought his potatoes either by the stone or half stone, at seven-pence to eight-pence the stone; of bacon he got now and then a pound; and perhaps every six or seven weeks he laid in as much as seven or eight pounds of shambles' meat. He had no ale this christmas or he would have drawn *me* a pot full; he had never brewed since his wife died, which was twelve months since last June. Butter he now bought by the pound or half pound; and cheese he never bought now, except sometimes a pennyworth for a taste; his flour he bought every week on credit, at two shillings and sixpence the dozen; and his coals he got by a tub at once, at one shilling and three-pence halfpenny the tub. He declared he never worked harder since he was wed than he does now. On my observing that the flannel manufacture was once a comfortable, homely business; he said it was; he could at one time send his children to school, whilst himself and wife remained at home at work; their quarter's bills for learning would come to as much as twenty-five, or twenty-six shillings, and he paid them willingly; he could do it then without embarrassing himself, but no working man could discharge such accounts in these times.

RADCLIFFE OLD HALL.

TO THE EDITOR OF THE MANCHESTER GUARDIAN.

Sir,

In your last Wednesday's number, an article is entitled " Radcliffe Old Hall," in which it is stated, that it was taken down to make room for a row of cottages. I should presume, on reading it, that Mr. Bamford had never visited the place, but spoke from hearsay. It fell down, and so far from being taken down to make room for a row of cottages, those alluded too don't stand upon any part of the ground formerly occupied by it. With respect to its being older than Haddon Hall, I am at a loss to conjecture upon what such an opinion is founded. Radcliffe Hall, with its two towers, (part of one is yet remaining) was built in the reign of Henry the Fourth, but there is no inconsiderable portion of Haddon at the present time, at least two centuries older. There is no ground, that I am aware of, to conclude that Radcliffe Hall was older than the fifteenth century. I grant there is an idea of its great antiquity in the immediate neighbourhood, and I was told upon the very spot, that it was fourteen hundred years old. If my informant had said *four,* it would have been much nearer the mark. It has been called, and certainly was, a manor-house of the first rank, and was once the seat of the Earl of Sussex, conspicuous in the time of Queen Elizabeth.

As the article in question is not historically correct, and reflects upon the taste of the Earl of Wilton, I have thought it proper to trouble you with a few remarks upon the subject, as I think the present owner has a proper regard for a valuable specimen of ancient domestic architecture, and that by means of your widely circulated journal, an improper idea may be formed of that nobleman.

I remain, your obedient servant,

S. HEYWOOD, Jun.

Walshaw Hall, near Bury.

[We readily give insertion to the above, as correcting some inaccuracies. Mr. Heywood need not be surprised at the traditional notion of the great antiquity of the building entertained in the neighbourhood; for there was a "William de Radeclive, of Radeclive Tower," in the thirteenth year of King John (A. D. 1281.) By letters patent from Henry the Fourth, (dated fifteenth of August, 1403,) James Radclyffe, of Radclyffe Tower, was empowered to rebuild a certain hall with two towers, and to kernel and embattle the walls, hall, and towers, and to hold the same as a for-talice to himself and his heirs for ever, As to the dilapidation of the edifice, Dr. Whittaker describes the old hall adjoining the tower, as existing in 1818, and says, " The two massive principals, which support the roof, are the most curious specimens of carved wood-work I have ever seen." He also notices " a moulded cornice of oak," " the remains of a very curious win-dow frame of oak, wrought in Gothic tracery," and " a door of massive oak, pointed at the top." Mr. Baines, in his History of Lancashire, states that in 1833, the " hall " was used as a hay-loft and cow-shed; and that nothing visible then remained of the moulded cornice of oak, the massive principals, ornamented pillars, pointed doorway, or curious oak frame, men-tioned by the learned doctor. He adds, " The prin-cipal part of the edifice, which stands within a few yards of the church, near a cluster of cottages, is a neglected ruin, and the remains of what may be pro-perly called the tower, partake of the general dilapida-tion." He also says that where buttresses were wanting, the walls. had fallen, and that part of the materials from the east and north sides of the building, as well as of the tower, had been used in the erection of a neighbouring corn-mill. In the " Illustrated Itinerary of the county of Lancaster," published in 1842, we find the following passage :—" The hall has now totally disappeared. An eye-witness described to us the process of its demolition with an indifference of the same nature as led to its removal. The only thing which seems to have excited his mind, was the massiveness of the timber which its destruction brought before his eyes. We can never cease to regret that these interesting memorials   *   *   should not, in the course of the vicissitudes of property, have come into the possession of persons more wishful to preserve their existence." From these extracts, we infer that, for want of protecting buttresses, some portions of the walls fell, but that beyond this, there has been a demolition by the owner. If this be an erroneous notion, it is one conveyed by the historians of the county, and should be controverted.—*Ed. Guard.*]

TO THE EDITOR OF THE MANCHESTER GUARDIAN.

Sir,

In your paper of Saturday last, I find that Mr. Heywood, of Walshaw, near Bury, contradicts my statement that Radcliffe old hall was, " taken down :" he says, " it fell down." Now the fact is, it was part of the building called, " the chapel," which was contiguous to the hall, that fell down. This took place about fourteen years ago, and the hall itself was taken down about two years afterwards.

He denies that the hall was taken down " to make room for a row of cottages," and in that he is partly right and partly wrong, as I have well ascertained ; it was not taken down " to make room for the cottages," but to build them. All the materials of the hall, which were convertible for the cottages were taken out, and built into them as wanted ; the cottages therefore do not stand on the exact site of the hall, but some eight or ten yards from it and in that respect, and that only does Mr. Heywood's representation disprove mine.

He seems to think I had never visited the place, but had taken my account from hearsay. I beg to assure him that I was on the spot when the old hall, and the old chapel were standing together, and that I was astonished, and deeply grieved, when, on my next visit, both were gone.

The chapel, or what was so termed by residents on the spot, was, as I have said, contigious to the hall, and was entered from it by a door : it was probably in this place, that Dr. Whittaker observed the " curious specimens of carved wood work," which you mention. Part of this room, or place, fell from neglect and dilapidation, and the timbers were ridded out, and carted away to some coal works on Cockey moor. The hall still remained, part of it occupied as four tenements, by four separate families, and other parts as a barn and cow-house, and it was these latter parts which I saw. Mrs. Bealey and sons wanted more dwellings for their work people, and the hall, under some contract or other, was pulled down to furnish materials to build them. "We pulled it down," said the contractor for the job, " and hard work we had of it :" so much for Mr. Heywood's assertion that it fell down.

Nine or ten cottages were builded, or part builded, from the materials, and a great quantity of timbers, all of black oak, and some of immense size and bulk remained after the cottages were completed; these timbers were taken to Mrs. Bealey and Sons' woodyard, where they were regarded as objects of curiosity by all who beheld them. One window frame in particular—as my informant said, but it was probably a door frame—was of most ponderous weight; several of the main supports were twenty feet in length, and two feet in thickness as they stood, and being made to curve, and join at the top, like a pointed arch, they must have been cut from trees of uncommon dimensions. The stairs to the chambers were cut from solid square blocks of oak, sawn down at the angles; all the other details were in keeping with these rude and massive materials, and as I gazed upon them in astonishment and awe—for I had never dreamed of there being such a place in our neighbourhood,—my thoughts were irresistibly hurried back to far remote times, when the wolf, and the deer, and the wild-boar ranged these lands, and when a forest almost would be felled to embattle, in a hold like this, one man against other hostile men. Nothing could possibly have more truly realized the description of the hall of Cedric the Saxon, as given by Sir Walter Scott, in his romance of Ivanhoe, than did this old hall at Radcliffe; and I do not see any reason whatever for not assigning to this part of the building, a Saxon origin. The name is Saxon; the family was, almost undoubtedly a Saxon one, as nearly all the old families in this part are; the place and its neighbourhood are still, eminently rife of Saxon customs, manners, and language; and in the midst of all these, finding a building with every characteristic of Saxon architecture, should we not be careful of denying it an origin to which it seems so naturally allied; a date which it so strongly claims.

Mr. Heywood says, " the hall and the towers were built in the reign of Henry the Fourth," whilst you show in your very lucid note, that there was " a William de Radeclive, of Radeclive Tower," one hundred and twenty-two years before Mr. Heywood's date. In 1403, " James Radclyffe," as you say, " was empowered to rebuild a certain hall with two towers, &c.," which shows that a hall, as well as towers, were, or had been, in existence before he was empowered to rebuild them. It does not follow that the whole of the hall and towers were then down, or were then rebuilt; nay, is it not most probable, that this James Radclyffe, would only rebuild what he pulled down, or found down, or dilapidated, and that, as a sensible man would now-a-days, he would preserve the best part of the old buildin, and occupy it whilst his alterations were going on, and then "kernel and embattle it" along with the new structure. Does not this reasoning lead us back, and present to our imagination the late hall as being the one which William de Radeclive would occupy in the reign of King John.—A. D. 1281—and does not that bring us to the verge of the period in which the scene of Ivanhoe is laid? the times of the latter Saxons, or early Norman chiefs?

I have not, nor had I, any wish whatever, in noticing this matter in my current publication to, "reflect upon the taste" of the noble owner of the property. I merely wished to give my description, furnished by memory, of what I had seen; and to express my regret, that a relic so deeply interesting,—and the more so from its being situated in a district where nothing else of the sort remained,—had not been deemed worthy of preservation.

I am, Sir,

Yours very respectfully,

Blakeley, July 24th, 1844.   SAMUEL BAMFORD.